Thorsons
PRINCIPLES
OF

WICCA

VIVIANNE CROWLEY

Thorsons

Thorsons
An Imprint of HarperCollins*Publishers*
77–85 Fulham Palace Road,
Hammersmith, London W6 8JB
1160 Battery Street
San Francisco, California 94111–1213

Published by Thorsons 1997

9 10 8

A catalogue record for this book
is available from the British Library

ISBN 0 7225 3451 5

Printed and bound in Great Britain by
Caledonian International Book Manufacturing, Glasgow

WICCA

IN THE SAME SERIES:

TO CHRIS, AS ALWAYS,
AND TO THOSE WITH WHOM WE JOURNEY.
BLESSÈD BE.

CONTENTS

INTRODUCTION

This book is for those who would like to know more about Wicca and for those who would like to try Wiccan practice for themselves. Often Wicca is a group activity and a book such as this cannot pretend to teach a would-be Witch everything he or she wants to know. However, it is a starting point which will allow you to explore for yourself some of the basic practices and concepts of Wicca. From here, you can decide whether it is something which you wish to pursue further or to integrate into your life.

Whatever you decide, learn and enjoy.

Happy exploring and blessèd be!

WHAT IS WICCA?

I f you go down to the woods today, you may have a big sur-
prise. In deep forests and grass-clad clearings, you may find
covens of Witches worshipping the ancient Pagan deities of
their lands and peoples; chanting, drumming, feasting and
rejoicing in the life that the Gods have given us. They may be
making magic to heal the Earth or those that are sick; they may
be practising the ancient arts of divination. They may be practising *Wicca*, the ancient art, craft and religion of Witchcraft.

Today, the words *Wicca, Shamanism, Witchcraft, Witch, Wise
Woman, Cunning Man, Magician* are often heard; but what do
they mean? *Wicca* is the religion of Witchcraft. Witchcraft is
not merely a system of magic. Within the Wiccan community,
Witchcraft has a capital letter and is used in a special sense. Wicca
is a Pagan mystery religion of Goddess and God. It is also a
Nature religion. It is not a remnant of the past and of the six-
teenth- and seventeenth-century Witch trials. Ancient though the
roots of this tradition are, it is alive and well in the world today.

My own Wiccan training was primarily in Britain, but since
then I have worked with Witches in North America, Australia
and all over Europe. Each country has its own Witchcraft traditions. These draw primarily on European traditions, but in the
case of the United States, for instance, they are influenced by

Native American spirituality and by West African traditions. Wicca is therefore a synthesis of a number of different belief systems that have endured into the modern age because they are relevant to our needs today.

The word *Wicca* itself is derived from the Anglo-Saxon word *Wicce*, a Witch. Originally this was pronounced *Witcha* but in modern times it is pronounced *Wicka*. The word *Witch* is a difficult one. It conjures images of the dark, the hag-like, the forbidden; the three Witches in William Shakespeare's play *Macbeth*; black candles, broomsticks, poisons, wax images with pins, incantations, 'hubble, bubble, toil and trouble', cauldrons, graveyards; many suspect things. There is also the image of the Witch as a vampire: a strong woman using her sexual energy to lure men into her power; just as in Greek myth the Witch Circe turned the hero Odysseus' men into swine.

Positive images of the Witch are more difficult to find, but they are there in folklore and children's stories. There is the *user-friendly* Granny – a nice elderly lady with silver-grey hair who lives in a cottage in the middle of the wood with a big black cat curled up by a warm fire. She is the Fairy Godmother whose magic wand heals all ills. There is the occasional TV Witch. Some people may remember or have seen re-runs of the television series *Bewitched*. This was one of my favourite television programmes as a child, but I could never see why the lovely Witch Samantha had married boring Darren or why she objected to doing housework by nose twitching. It seemed a very sensible idea to me.

Some Witch images are positive, others negative; but they have common threads. These give us the first clues on our quest to discover who and what Witches really are: the Witch is a magic-maker and Witches worship a Goddess – the Great Mother Goddess. They also worship the Horned God. In Greek mythology he is Pan and, to the Celts, Herne or Cernunnos. In other words, Witchcraft is a religion. It is a pre-Christian religion originating in the mists of time. It is based on remnants of simple Pagan traditions handed down in folklore and country custom. Onto these have been grafted more sophisticated beliefs from the more formal Paganisms of Rome, Greece and Egypt, and from the initiatory mystery traditions. Wicca involves the development of magical psychic powers; but hand in hand with the wisdom to use them. An initiatory system of spiritual development is an intrinsic part of the tradition.

WHO ARE TODAY'S WITCHES?

Who are they, these people who call themselves *Witches*, who walk the ancient ways, who work the traditional magics, who speak once more to long-silent Goddesses and Gods? They are men and women of all nations and races. They are young, old, rich, poor. They are those who have woken up to the fact that material creation is not the be all and end all; that science does not have all the answers; nor do the so-called *world religions*. They have remembered something which many of us have forgotten. Partly it is ancient wisdom; partly it is common sense.

People come to Wicca for many reasons. Some seek occult power and knowledge. Some are drawn to Wicca by feminism and the role of the Goddess; others by ecological awareness and reverence for Nature; still others seek spiritual transformation.

Magic is an attraction for some. Gerald Gardner, one of the 'founding fathers' or revivers of modern Wicca once wrote:

> Witchcraft was, and is, not a cult for everybody. Unless you have
> an attraction to the occult, a sense of wonder, a feeling that you
> can slip for a few minutes out of the world into the world of faery,
> it is of no use to you.[1]

4   Many people come to Wicca because they already see themselves as Witches. We may have had a sense of an inner power
that had no name; a sense that just beyond the realm of sight
and sound and touch there dwelt another kingdom – the *Land
of Faery*. Perhaps we went there in our dreams.

Some of us were aware that some of this *Faery Power* dwelt
within us. Perhaps we had precognitive dreams. Sometimes we
knew the future. We may have tried to develop this by working
with tarot cards and telling the fortunes of our friends. Perhaps
we were scared when our predictions came true and stopped
looking into the misty glass of the future. Perhaps we found we
had the power of small magics. We could wish for something
very hard and it would come true. Perhaps we found books of
spellcraft on the shelves of our library or bookstore and tried
them. Maybe when we talked to our relatives we found that
some of our family had the *sight*. Perhaps our grandmother told
fortunes using tea leaves, or our grandfather dreamt the family
deaths the day before they occurred. Perhaps we had an aunt
who was a medium, a grandfather who was a spiritual healer,
a great grandmother who was a herbalist and cured the community in days when no one could afford a doctor unless someone was at death's door.

This heritage of power and sight may have been manifest in us
from childhood, but we may have had no outlet for it; or perhaps
it was discouraged. Perhaps it manifested in our teenage years,
when often teenagers have what is called *psychokinetic* energy.
Lights flicker when we walk by, photocopiers grind to a halt;
vases mysteriously leap off shelves and smash themselves at our
feet. Often our families have no explanations for these things, so
we have to seek explanations elsewhere. Perhaps we come upon
books of magic, tarot, astrology, divination, healing. We may find
that the religious framework we were taught as children has no
place for these arts, but there is a religious framework that does.

This is the religious framework of Wicca. In the early years of the Wiccan revival, most people came through the occult route; perhaps because other important aspects of Wicca were less well known. Today things are very different.

For women, Wicca is a spiritual path in which we can worship the Divine in its female form – as Goddess. Many women come to Wicca from feminism. They have re-evaluated the word *Witch* and realized that it involves the use of the innate powers of the Wise Woman. The Wise Woman was the traditional village midwife. (In French, midwives are still call *sages femmes, wise women*.) For those of you familiar with the tarot, the Wise Woman has affinity with the Queen of Pentacles – a very Earthy lady! Other women might consider the role of the Wiccan priestess attractive, allowing them to fulfil a spiritual role usually denied them in Western society today.

It is not only women who seek the Goddess. Men too are attracted by Wicca's vision of deity as both Goddess and God. In the popular mind, Witches are female and this can be a barrier to men interested in Wicca. However, both men and women are Witches. A male Witch is simply that – not a warlock or a wizard. The idea that Witches are always women is a relatively new one. At the height of the Witchcraft persecutions in Europe and America, both men and women were killed and when I came into Wicca in England a quarter of a century ago, there were more male than female Witches. It is more difficult for men to identify with the word *Witch*, but here are some ways of thinking about it. The traditional male Witch is a countryman. He is one who is in touch with the elements, who has worked the land, healed a bird's broken wing or the illness of a child; one who loves the Goddess and knows both Goddess and God, whatever any church might tell him.

Another route to Wicca is through the growing environmental awareness in society today. Wicca honours the Divine as manifest in Nature. The Earth is our spiritual mother and we sense that the Divine is not 'out there' but all around us. Nature itself is sacred and holy, a manifestation of the Divine Life Force. Greenpeace, environmental action, vegetarianism, animal rights, are all manifestations of a reawakening spirit of reverence towards the Earth. This was natural and instinctive to our ancestors, but recent centuries of urban living have suppressed it.

Initiation, in the sense of a personal transformatory experience of the Divine, is undoubtedly an attraction of Wicca for some. Some Wiccan traditions have three or more initiation ceremonies that mark transitions through spiritual change. Such rites can be powerful spiritual and psychological events that are life-enhancing and life-changing.

COVENS AND COMMUNITY

Unless you live in Salem, Massachusetts, site of the worst Witch persecutions in the United States and today centre of a thriving Witch tourist industry, you will not see Witches in black robes and pointed hats in your local supermarket. This is not because Witches prefer a diet of eye of newt and toe of frog, or that they do not do mundane things like shopping. However, for the most part, Witches today are much like everyone else; although they tend to be better educated than average. Some Witches are authors and teachers and spend all their time writing about and teaching the Craft; others are full-time healers or tarot readers. However, most Witches have conventional jobs. Certain professions attract Witches more than others. In the United States, information technology is popular; ironically the followers of the Old Religion are at the leading edge of high technology. In Europe, health care and social workers; artists, musicians and actors; and teachers and lecturers are the three biggest groupings.

Some Witches are solo Witches. Others belong to covens. Covens are stable groups of like-minded people who meet together to worship the Gods and do magic. They may also engage in social, environmental and teaching activities. The classic number of people in a coven is thirteen; more than this and groups become unwieldy and difficult to manage. However, many covens are smaller. Groups of five to nine can be very effective. Some are mixed sex groups; others cater for Witches who prefer single sex covens. Some Witches belong not to small covens but to training schools or coven networks which have hundreds of members. Whatever the size of the group though, it is important to remember that Wicca is not something which other people do for you, but something that you do for yourself. If we practise our Wicca solo that is obvious, but it is also the case in a group situation. Rites are participatory and emphasize the Divine within all.

Some Witches are trained by individual Witches and others come into Wicca through a coven operating an initiatory system. In some cases Witches come from Witch families, but most come from outside the tradition. They feel they are drawn to Wicca or are natural Witches seeking to make contact with teachers who can help them develop along the path. There are books through which it is possible to learn much. Books can add to our store of knowledge but it is difficult to learn Wicca from books alone. Learning Wicca is like learning anything else: at some stage we need to practise with others to improve our skill and knowledge and to assess how good we really are. Wicca is also a bit like learning a language. We can read books, listen to tapes, but in the end we need to speak that language with others to know how to use it.

Each coven has teachings derived from the accumulated generations who have worked in that particular coven. If it is part of an initiatory tradition, it will also have the core material of

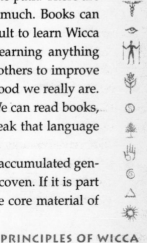

the tradition. This is recorded in a book of rites and spells, the *Book of Shadows*. Computers notwithstanding, each Witch must make his or her own handwritten copy. Wicca is part of the modern world, but it is also an inheritor of past traditions.

ORIGINS OF WICCA

Wicca's history is that of natural magic, the Pagan mystery traditions, such as those of Egypt and Eleusis, and of Celtic spirituality. Wicca draws on mysticism, astrology, runes, tarot and, in modern times, on insights from psychology. It also draws on the traditions of healing of body and of soul.

Although the Wiccan practice I describe here is European in origin, Wicca represents universal and fundamental beliefs and skills. Similar traditions exist all over the world; wherever native indigenous spirituality has not been suppressed. We find similar ideas in North America, South America, Africa, Asia, Polynesia, everywhere where people have sought to honour the Divine and to use the innate powers of the human psyche.

The Wiccan revival in the twentieth century began in England, sacred Albion, home of Glastonbury, Stonehenge and the legends of the Grail. This is perhaps no accident. The idea that the Western islands of Europe were Holy Ground and sacred soil is a long-held tradition. The greatest Druid training schools in the Celtic era were in Britain and Ireland. In Medieval times, scholars claimed that Britain was given to their ancestors by the Goddess Diana. In 1136, the historian Geoffrey of Monmouth described in his *History of the Kings of Britain* how refugees escaping in pre-Christian times from the siege of Troy were desperately seeking a new homeland. Their leader called upon Diana to help them:

O powerful Goddess,
terror of the forest glades,
yet hope of the wild woodlands,
you, who have the power to go in orbit,
through the airy heavens and the halls of hell,
pronounce a judgement which concerns the Earth.
Tell me which lands you wish us to inhabit.
Tell me of a safe dwelling-place
where I am to worship you down the ages,
and where, to the chanting of maidens,
I shall dedicate temples to you.

This he said nine times; four times he proceeded round the altar, pouring the wine which he held upon the sacrificial hearth; then he lay down upon the skin of a hind which he had stretched before the altar. Having sought for slumber, he at length fell asleep.

It was then about the third hour of the night, when mortal beings succumb to the sweetest rest; that it seemed to him the Goddess stood before him and spoke these words to him:

Brutus, beyond the setting of the Sun,
past the realms of Gaul,
there lies an island in the sea,
once occupied by giants.
Now it is empty and ready for your folk.[2]

These Pagan links are part of the reason why Witchcraft has revived most quickly in England rather than in other parts of Europe. Another is England's remoteness from Rome. This meant that it was Christianized later than some parts of Europe and with the Protestant Reformation could more easily break from Rome. English Protestantism was not a fanatical variety. It did not engage in Witch persecutions with the same enthusiasm as some of its Catholic and Protestant neighbours. English Protestantism was a curious hybrid of moderate Catholicism and Lutheranism in a church headed not by a religious figure but by the monarch – the King or Queen. This Church of England was a state church whose interests were as much about creating a stable society as about religion.

On the fringes of Western Europe many Pagan ideas endured in ways they could not elsewhere. Other than Celtic Brittany in North-west France, Britain and Ireland are the parts of Europe where Pagan sacred sites have best survived. Scottish, Welsh, English and Irish cultures all show their Pagan origins. Scratch the surface and you will find village customs such as May-pole dancing, well-dressing, the Abbots Bromley Horn Dance, Morris Men, Harvest festivals – all remnants of Pagan religious customs.

People often think of Europe as having being Christian for two thousand years, but this is not the case. Paganism and Christianity were still struggling over a thousand years later. Medieval laws tell us much about Paganism because they tell us what it was necessary to suppress. This included making offerings to non-Christian Gods, performing Witchcraft or divination, swearing vows at wells, trees or stones, and gathering herbs with non-Christian incantations. In the eleventh century when King Canute issued laws against *Heathenism* or Paganism, this is what he forbade.

> We earnestly forbid every Heathenism:
> Heathenism is, that men worship idols;
> that is, that they worship Heathen Gods,
> and the Sun or the Moon,
> fire or rivers,
> water-wells or stones,

or forest trees of any kind;

or love Witchcraft.[3]

Witchcraft and Paganism survived in rural areas as part of the folk traditions and folk medicine of the people. This does not mean that the ruling classes of society were not exposed to these folk traditions. Communal festivities such as May Day were celebrated by both high and low.

Witches were consulted by all strata of British society well into the nineteenth century. Hannah Green of Yeadon in Yorkshire, known as the 'Ling Bob Witch', inherited her mother's practice which she ran for forty years. In 1810, she left a thousand pounds in her will, an enormous sum of money in those days. Cunning Murrell, who died in 1860, was a male witch from Essex who practised healing, averting the evil eye, astrology, herbalism, and spellcraft for clients as far away as London. After his death he was found to have owned a trunkful of books and manuscripts including magical texts from the seventeenth century.

Witchcraft and Pagan religious traditions survived in rural areas, but Witchcraft would have remained an underground tradition if it was not for the work of one man, Gerald Gardner, who became familiar to many thousands of people through his radio broadcasts, books and media publicity. He was one of the first Witches in the twentieth century to talk publicly about his beliefs and to share them with others. Most photographs show him in later life, with a white goatee beard looking for all the world like an elderly Pan. Gerald Gardner spent most of his adult working life away from Europe in far flung outposts of the British Empire. He was able to study and get to know the indigenous peoples and further his interest in folklore, naturism, Pagan religions and Witchcraft. When Gerald Gardner retired to England in the 1930s, he

made contact with a coven of English Witches. These Witches met in the New Forest, an ancient royal hunting ground of the Norman kings in southern England. The coven had a system of initiation not dissimilar to the three degrees of Freemasonry. The group practised spell-making, ritual and worship. Their rituals celebrated a seasonal myth cycle. Just how ancient the tradition was is a subject of much debate. Nevertheless, Gerald Gardner's two most well known books *Witchcraft Today* (1954) and *The Meaning of Witchcraft* (1959) produced a huge surge of interest, inspiring a movement that has spread around the world.

ASPECTS OF WICCA

Wicca has many aspects. To help us understand these we can divide them into five branches. These relate to what are known as the 'Elements of the Wise'. In magical philosophy, these make up the whole of creation – Earth, Air, Fire, Water and Ether or Spirit. Ether or Spirit, the fifth non-material element, is that which binds the other four together, but which is greater than the sum of their parts.

The pentagram is a symbol strongly associated with Witches; sometimes with sinister connotations. However, there is nothing sinister about it. The pentagram is the five-pointed star that represents the five Elements. It is also a symbol of the perfected human being. The four Elements of material creation are surmounted by the fifth Element of Spirit – the Element that links us to the Divine.

In the Western magical tradition, each point of the pentagram relates to a particular Element. The symbols beside each point of the pentagram are the alchemical symbols for the Element.

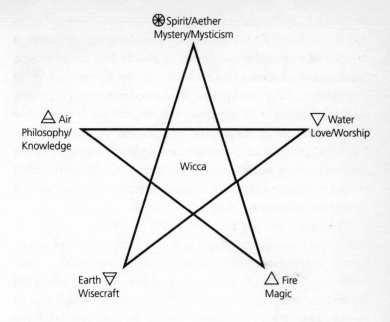

The Wiccan Pentagram

Air in magical tradition relates to the mind, intellect, word, thought, philosophy, our ideas about the universe and our world view. Fire equates with energy, passion, will – in Wicca the magical powers. Water is the Element of love, that which unites and binds us to others and to the universe around us. It is from love that our worship of the Gods, our respect for one another and our veneration of Nature springs. Water represents the religious element in Wicca. Wisecraft is Earth – the practical knowledge of the Wise Woman and Cunning Man that was the precursor of modern science. Spirit represents Wicca as an initiatory Mystery Tradition, the mystical aspect of Wicca.

This book is about these five aspects of Wicca. It does not tell you how to run a coven, but it talks about the basis of Wicca –

how to begin to create a magical and spiritual life. Wicca is about many things but in particular it is about love and respect – love and respect for the Earth, its people, our environment, those near and dear to us and for ourselves. It is also about empowerment – about learning to use our energies and powers wisely and well. It is about growth and change – a spiritual growth and change that take us nearer the source of our being, the Gods. It is about harmony and rhythms: attuning to the cycle of seasons and change within our own lives and outside in the universe, and finding a sense of inner peace and harmony by becoming aware that we are part of a greater whole.

These ideas are not peculiar to Wicca. They are within all spiritual and magical traditions. Each tradition, however, speaks in its own language and symbols and has its own emphases. The Wiccan tradition speaks in the language of the Western mystery and magical tradition, some of which will be familiar to people from astrology. It also speaks in the language of Paganism – its deities are Pagan Goddesses and Gods. Wicca speaks therefore to those who recognize that the Divine does not choose to manifest itself in only one form and through a single revelation. It is constantly showing itself to us through different images until at last we understand the whole. Wicca also speaks to those for whom the energy of the Goddess is as important as that of a male God. It speaks, in short, to modern men and women who love the Earth, for whom women and men are equal, and who can respect the traditions of others while valuing and revering their own. In other words, Wicca speaks to the Wise.

All this can sound very serious but it is important to remember that while Wicca has much in common with other religions, there are important differences. To many people the word *religion* implies impractical ideas about sex and contraception, boring church services, a ridiculous set of beliefs,

being a killjoy and going around telling other people what not
to do. Wicca is a religion that celebrates the joy of being alive,
the beauty of nature, the miracle of existence and consciousness, the gifts that Nature gives us. It involves solemnity but
also mirth – drumming, chanting, dancing, feasting and above
all fun. People are Wiccan because they enjoy it. In Wicca we
follow the way of the Bodhisattva and not the way of the
Buddha. We are interested in the world and seek to change it
and not to flee it or retreat from it.

Let us look therefore at the Wiccan universe. But before clut-
tering up the brain with more words, you might like to try a
simple exercise.

SIMPLE EXERCISES TO BEGIN

At the end of each chapter there will be an exercise to help you
appreciate an aspect of Wicca. The first exercise is the Meadow
Exercise. This is an exercise which can prepare us for magical or
ritual work, or it can be a meditative exercise in itself. It is energizing as well as relaxing. You can try it when you come home to
help switch off from the work tensions and to focus on your private life. Alternatively, you can do it just before you go to bed to
clear your mind for sleep. If you feel depressed or anxious, you
can use the exercise to help you get your problems into perspective. Against the backcloth of the timeless world of Nature, our
individual concerns assume their true perspective – important,
yes, but not so important in the greater scheme of things. Keep a
notebook recording your experiences with these exercises. This
will help you monitor your progress.

Once you are familiar with the exercise, you will find that you
can do it whenever you have a quiet moment – sitting at your
desk at work, sitting at the kitchen table while waiting for a pan
to boil, in the college library, in the odd gap between patients.

CONTACTING THE ELEMENTS IN NATURE:
THE MEADOW VISUALIZATION

1. Begin by sitting quietly in your room. Let all the tensions and the stresses of the day flow away from you and fade away.

2. Still yourself and let your breathing become deeper and more relaxed. As your breathing deepens, focus on it. Let your mind become more calm and let it dwell in the internal peace of your own rhythmic breath. Remain like this until you feel calm and receptive.

3. Now imagine that the walls of your room are slowly dissolving away. You find yourself sitting in a sunny meadow. The grass is thick, green and lush around you. The earth feels warm and comforting beneath.

4. The sun shines down above you. Its rays warm you. A light wind blows against you and caresses your face. Close by you hear the sound of running water as it flows along in a stream.

5. You become aware that you are surrounded by the four elements – Wind (Air), Sun (Fire), Water, Earth; each one supporting, comforting or energizing you in a different way.

6. Now you become aware that these elements are but different forms of energy; the energy that is the life force.

7. Focus on your breath again and imagine it is also the life force. Each breath is an intake of life force energy.

8. Feel your breath, not only as air rushing into your lungs but also as the life force itself. Feel it flowing through your body.

9. Sense yourself becoming a being of energy. Sense the energy of the world ebbing and flowing and pulsating all around you; running through you and around you. You are it and it is you.

10. Hold this image for a little while – perhaps for a couple of minutes – and then let the energy that has been building up within you slowly subside.

11. Return to everyday awareness and when you feel ready to get up, do so.
12. Take your time and try not to make any sudden or hurried movements for a little while.
13. Make a note of your experiences: how difficult or easy you found it to concentrate, how you felt at different stages of the exercise. While writing up your notes, you will find it helpful to eat and drink something. This will *earth* you. It will bring you fully into everyday awareness and centre you in your body.

The meadow you have created in your visualization is your own safe space. It is somewhere you can go whenever you feel the need for tranquillity and safety. At this stage, do not try to leave your meadow.

Notes

1. Gerald B Gardner, *Witchcraft Today*, Rider & Co, London 1954, page 29.
2. Geoffrey of Monmouth, *The History of the Kings of Britain*, Lewis Thorpe (trans), Penguin, Harmondsworth 1966, page 65.
3. *Laws of King Cnut*, quoted in Margaret A Murray, *The Witch-Cult in Western Europe: A Study in Anthropology*, Clarendon Press, Oxford 1921, page 23.

THE WICCAN UNIVERSE

The Wiccan universe is a holistic universe. All of creation is alive. People, animals, plants, trees, rocks, crystals, molecules, even atoms, have their own purposes and spiritual force. They are entities or organisms. This is not just a romantic anthropomorphism created to sustain us through the *angst* of human life. Material creation is infinitely more mysterious than our everyday awareness tells us. Our sense receptors have evolved to show us that a table is a table – no more and no less.

We do not have to view it as a collection of moving molecules teeming with atoms like a giant ant hill of activity. However, this might be nearer the truth. Many of the ways in which we perceive the universe are an illusion. When we look out into the sky at night we see an emptiness filled with planets and stars, but the dark spaces are not empty. They are full of something which physicists call *dark matter*. This is the dark remnants of stars, black holes and particles as yet unknown to physics. Dark matter fills more than ninety per cent of the universe. Dark matter is not only out there in space. It is all around us. Scientists can tell of its existence because of the tiny magnetic interactions of its particles and its effect on gravitational fields. Our universe is infinitely mysterious and our understanding of it is only just beginning.

In our holistic universe, it is not only the animal, plant and mineral life of our planet that is alive. It is the planet itself. This idea was developed by Otter (also known as Tim or Oberon) Zell of the Pagan *Church of All Worlds*, but more famously by distinguished scientist James Lovelock in his *Gaia Hypothesis*.[1] James Lovelock is the inventor of the microwave. He was the first person to measure CFC gases and to observe that our ozone layer was becoming depleted. He believes that the Earth is a living being. His idea evolved when he started thinking about ways of detecting life on Mars. If the Earth's atmosphere consisted of gases in chemical equilibrium, like the atmospheres of Mars and Venus, it would be 99 per cent carbon dioxide. Instead, the Earth has an atmosphere with very little carbon dioxide, 21 per cent oxygen and 78 per cent nitrogen. Oxygen and nitrogen are produced by the living organisms that inhabit the Earth. Bacteria release nitrogen and plants photosynthesize releasing oxygen. Plankton in the oceans remove carbon from the atmosphere and turn it into their tiny shells. When the plankton die, their shells fall to the sea bed. Here they are converted into the calcium carbonate found in limestone

PRINCIPLES OF WICCA

rocks. Together, plants, animals and minerals interact in such a way as to seem part of a living being, a greater whole. This is the *biosphere*, or *Gaia*. James Lovelock's *Gaia Hypothesis* is the scientific recognition of what Witches and magicians have always known: that the Earth is alive. It is a balanced, integrated, self-regulating system working in such close harmony that it acts like a single being. This then is how Wicca sees our world – fascinating, interacting, mysterious and alive.

THE ELEMENTS OF THE WISE

Holism is both the leading edge of science and the view of ancient mysticism. In Wicca we often find the symbol of the *Spiral Dance*: we move on only to return to the point at which we started, but not in exactly the same place. The experience of the journey has given us a new perspective and starting point. Thus it is with science and the magical view of the universe.

Within our interacting holistic universe, there are many different types of energy. There are many ways of categorizing them. All spiritual traditions have different ways of looking at the universe. In a sense all these systems and categories are artificial. In reality, nothing is wholly one thing, wholly another, but is a combination of many things. However, in the magical universe an ancient Greek idea still works well. This is the idea mentioned in Chapter 1 that the material universe consists of energy in four basic states – Earth, Air, Fire and Water. Beyond material creation is a fifth state – Ether or Spirit. Here are some ideas about the elements.

AIR

In magical tradition, Air is the realm of mind, the brain, the intellect and logical linear thought. The Airy side of us is the part that wants to learn, which is curious and tries to understand the true nature of things. It is youthful, light and energetic. Air can be quickness of thought, lightness of being, humour, the joy of life. The tarot card of the Fool springs to mind. This is ruled by Air and represents a stepping out into the unknown with joy; although this can be dangerous.

There is an excitement in Air. It values the new and untried. Air always wants to learn new things whatever the price. Air signs are good at starting anew, and at throwing old things away. Much more so than Earth and Water, though perhaps Fire rivals Air here. Air divides things into categories. It separates one thing from another. It gets to the point and is not 'woolly-minded'. Computers, library classification systems, indeed all systems, are Air-related. Objectivity is something which can be developed by working with the Air element.

Air is impersonal and detached; for emotion can distort our thinking processes. Air adheres to the letter of the law. Islamic Sharia law is a totally logical system. There is a list of crimes and a fixed set of penalties. Everyone knows exactly where they stand and, theoretically, the same treatment is meted out to all. This may be logical but it does not take account of another aspect of reality – individual circumstances. It is hard-nosed rather than soft in its approach.

One image of the Air-dominated person is that of Doctor Frankenstein. Here we have the mad professor in his laboratory, indulging in experiments that violate all important human values. His rationality has made him blind to other important aspects of reality. He forgets to eat and neglects his family in pursuit of the one goal that matters to him – learning.

The zodiac signs ruled by Air are Aquarius the Water-Bearer, symbol of the New Age, Libra the Scales, and Gemini the Twins.

FIRE

Fire gives warmth, sexuality, and warms the blood. Fire is activity, making things happen, excitement, entertainment, liveliness, the swiftness of the arrow.

Fire is important if we are to act in the world. It is a renewing and purifying element. After forest fires have burned the ground, all sorts of new life forms emerge. Fire transforms, transmutes, changes, destroys, but creates the ground for new growth. Fire is also associated with a hot temper which is part of its martial or war-like aspect. Fire can provoke arguments, but brings us energy and new life and vigour. It is also the hearth Fire and the Sun on a summer's day after long winter. The discovery of how to make fire was one of the greatest of human achievements and essential for the creation of civilization. It led to cooking, which has enabled us to enrich and broaden our diet. Cooking itself is rather like alchemy – a process of transmutation and change.

Fire is flamboyant and colourful. Fire's passion can foster our love of life, creativity, indignation against injustice. Fire is freedom and passion; the energy and the warmth of love as well as the desire to consume. The risk-taking theme is another aspect of Fire – courage or recklessness depending on which way one views it. Fire is impatient. Once it gets going it does not stop until it has burned itself out. This is certainly true of Fire sign people on the whole.

We often relate intuition to fire. Insight and inspiration can come like the arrows of Sagittarius from out of nowhere to jolt us out of our rut!

Its zodiac signs are all or part animal – Aries the Ram, Leo the Lion, and Sagittarius the Archer.

WATER

Water is fluid, accepting and tolerant. Water overcomes difficulties by flowing around them and ignoring them, instead of

all those organs associated with the emotions. It brings tears of
joy and tears of sorrow. It is love, compassion, the quality of
mercy, which, as Shakespeare wrote, '... is not strained but fall-
eth as the gentle rain of heaven upon the place beneath.' It is
the sea, dreaming and broody. It is the negative side of dreaming – fears and phobias. It unites others but can overwhelm
them. It can be the 'wet blanket'.

In Celtic mythology, Water was the gate to the Otherworld.
The Celts also associated Water with a return to the source. The
salmon of knowledge that swims upstream to its birth place
to spawn was revered in Celtic mythology. Interestingly, in
dreams and symbolism, the fish often appears as a symbol of
the Self, so the link with the return to the origin is appropriate.

Water has the power of erosion – it can wear away rock. It
can wear away opposition. The power of Water can overcome
all things – even our planet, if we insist on melting our ice caps
and raising our sea levels. Water can be a deep well of knowledge – the knowledge that comes from meditation and getting
in touch with the deepest unconscious part of ourselves, rather
than book knowledge. Empathy is another Water quality – the
ability to have insight into others and to feel their joy and pain.
Zodiac signs are Scorpio the Scorpion, Cancer the Crab and
Pisces the Fish.

EARTH

This is the element of the physical body, our flesh and bones.
Earth is the basis of material existence. Earth has the qualities
of steadfastness, dependability, endurance, protection. It is the
tortoise as opposed to the hare. It is realistic and all manner of
practical 'down to earth' things. However, it also has a more
pleasurable side. It is sex and sensuality, too much so sometimes. Earth can also be greedy about food and money.

Earth is an important element in Pagan initiatory rites. The cave paintings of our Stone Age ancestors had magical purposes and probably initiatory purposes as well. They were reached only by difficult and dark journeys through caverns lit by flickering torch light that made the pictures themselves seem alive. Here young people were told the myths of their tribe; stories that linked the tribe to its Gods and explained the mysteries of life and death, the origin of the universe and of the tribe itself. In the more sophisticated Paganism of ancient Greece, initiatory rites continued in the caves of Eleusis. Here in the rites dedicated to the Goddess, the Earth Mother, initiates were taught the mystery of life after death.

Gardening is a very earthy activity, as are sculpting and some of the other crafts. It is good to get in touch with our sensation function by manipulating matter. Earth is associated with stored wisdom. This is literally true because much of our knowledge of the past comes from archaeological artefacts stored under the Earth. There can be a great sense of peace in Earth meditations, but it is important to remember the destructive potential of Earth. However, Earth is patient. She can endure and rectify our mistakes – though it will take time. Earth zodiac signs are Taurus the Bull, Virgo the Virgin, and Capricorn the Goat.

In order to understand and practise Wicca, we need to get in touch with the energies of the elements around us. In other words, to get in touch with the Universe itself. Below are some simple exercises to help us tune into the Wiccan universe – a world of life and energy.

EXPERIENCING THE ELEMENTS

1. Wicca is an earth-based religion, so it is important for you to tune in to the natural world and the seasonal cycle. Spend two days doing as much as you can to experience the physical presence of all four elements. Get outside as often as you can. Walk upon, touch, dig, smell, feel the earth. Feel the sun against your skin, the wind against your face. Paddle in a stream, walk in the rain, swim in the sea.

2. Note the quality of the Earth on which you walk, the Air you breathe, the Water you drink or which falls on you as rain, the Sun that warms you. Meditate on what these elements might be saying to you. Are there things that you can learn from the way they operate in the world? How do they feel about their relationship with humankind?

3. To feel the Earth and its energy, try placing your hand on the ground and feeling the 'pulse' or 'heart beat' of the Earth. Inside the Earth is teeming with life – worms, insects, other small creatures, the growing of roots and upward thrusting of shoots. Although seemingly static, there is a constant movement within it. Also there is the movement of its geomagnetic fields. The Earth element is rich and abundant. Walking and hiking are good ways of making contact with it. Earth is also rocks and standing stones and cliffs: if you have access to any of these, visit them. Put the palms of your hands against them and feel their energy.

4. If you are stuck in an inner city concrete jungle, go to a city park. If this is impossible, walk the streets and try to connect with the earth beneath the layers of concrete. Sense what the Earth is feeling. If you are not able to go out, use a bowl of earth or perhaps a stone. Hold it and feel its qualities while you meditate on it.

5. Similarly with the other elements: Water is seas and rivers and pools and rain. Again, if you cannot get out, meditate on a bowl of water.

6. Air is, of course, the wind. Feel it against you, both physically and through meditation, in all its forms; from gentle zephyr breezes to the majesty and power of a gale. The mountains or any high place (even a tower block) are a good place to experience the power of Air.

7. With Fire, you may be able to light a camp fire. Be careful here though. If you make a fire, keep it under proper control and put it out afterwards. If it is impractical for you to light a fire outside and you have no hearth at home, remember that Fire is also the Sun. You can also meditate on Fire by burning a candle.

8. Keep a symbol of each element in your home: a bowl of earth and one of water; a candle for Fire; for Air, something light like a bird's feather or something which makes sounds such as wind chimes. Keep these together in a special place that can then become the basis for an altar.

9. Spend a day meditating on each of these elements. You may wish to ponder on the enormity, power and range of each. All are essential to support us, but their power is such that they can easily brush us aside and destroy us. Water is the tranquil stream, but also the raging sea. Fire can warm us but it can also be the inferno that destroys all in its path. Earth supports us but can quake, slide, slip or crumble away beneath our feet. Air can be the gentle breeze or the unstoppable hurricane.

10. Which elements do you feel you have in abundance in your personality? Which do you need to develop and why?

11. Record all your thoughts and insights on the elements. Remember to 'earth' yourself after each meditative exercise by eating and drinking something.

1. A Wiccan altar usually has symbols of all four elements on it, but there may be times in your life when you need to encourage the energy of one particular element into your life.

2. One way of doing this is to make an altar for the element that is lacking in your life. If you lack energy and are timid and unconfident, make a Fire altar. Use a red altar cloth, red flowers, a red-leafed potted plant, berries, red candles. To represent Earth, find a piece of red sandstone or other red rock. Use a bowl of red glass for your Water. For Air, burn an incense that seems hot and fiery. Place some tarot cards from the suite of wands on the altar if you have them.

3. Having set up your altar, light the candles and incense. Sit in front of the altar and meditate on how and where you can bring Fire into your life. Ask the powers of Fire to help you use them wisely and well in their appropriate place, but not in excess. Spend some time every day for a week meditating upon fire.

4. In the second week, take the fire energy into your everyday life. Put something from your fire altar such as your red rock or plant in your workplace. Wear something red when you need to display your fire energy. Take to using a red pen! All these are simple things but they are working on the age-old magical principle of sympathetic magic.

5. Similarly, if you need to display more love and sympathy, make a Water altar. If you need to sharpen your thinking use Air. To bring stability, inner strength and peace into your life, work with the element of Earth. For a Water altar, you could find a piece of cloth which seemed in colour and texture to be watery. You could add bowls of water in glass of watery shades and you could float a candle on one, a flower on another. You could add shells. For Air you could

use light colours, the colours of the sky, and feathers. For Earth, you need the colours of the Earth and of green and growing things.

Note

1. James Lovelock, *Gaia: A New Look at Life on Earth*, Oxford University Press, Oxford 1979.

NATURE AND SEASONS

Raw and cold is icy spring,
cold will arise in the wind;
the ducks of the watery pool have raised a cry,
passionately wailful is the harsh-shrieking crane
which the wolves hear in the wilderness at the early rise of morning;
birds awaken from meadows,
many are the wild creatures from which they flee
out of the wood,
out of the green grass.

A good season is summer for long journeys;
quiet is the tall fine wood,
which the whistle of the wind will not stir;
green is the plumage of the sheltering wood;
eddies swirl in the stream;
good is the warmth in the turf.

A good season for staying is autumn;
there is work then for everyone before the very short days.
Dappled fawns from amongst the hinds,
the red clumps of the bracken shelter them;
stags run from the knolls at the belling of the deer-herd.
Sweet acorns in the wide woods,
corn-stalks around the cornfields over the expanse of the brown earth.
There are thorn-bushes and prickly brambles by the midst of the
   ruined court;
the hard ground is covered with heavy fruit.
Hazel-nuts of good crop fall from the huge old trees on dykes.

In the black season of deep winter
a storm of waves is roused along the expanse of the world.
Sad are the birds of every meadow plain,
except the ravens that feed on crimson blood,
at the clamour of harsh winter;
rough, black, dark, smoky.
Dogs are vicious in cracking bones;
the iron pot is put on the fire after the dark black day.

IRISH, 11TH CENTURY, ATTRIBUTED TRADITIONALLY TO AMERGIN[1]

Attuning ourselves to the seasonal cycle is one of the most
important things about becoming a Witch. This may seem sur-
prising. After all, our Witch images were all of cats, capes and
cauldrons. Why do Witches celebrate seasonal festivals? Wicca

is a Nature religion. The Divine is in-dwelling in Nature and Nature is its cloak and garment. By celebrating the seasonal festivals we reconnect with the rhythms of Nature and we reconnect with the Divine. This can help end the sense of alienation and *anomie* felt by many in modern industrial society. It takes us back to our natural origins.

Our attitudes to Nature have evolved rapidly over recent centuries. The animist ideas of indigenous peoples and traditional societies – that Nature is alive – clashed with Western capitalism's scientific materialism. This declared that living creatures were like machines. There was no spiritual dimension to the universe. Nature was *natural resources*; something to be exploited, regardless of the consequences.

Mining, logging, deforestation, the lowering of the water table, all these short-term economic benefits were pursued at the expense of the long-term viability of our planet. Nature was seen as available for human exploitation; we were in control. We were wrong. The powers of the elements are not under our control. We cannot hold back the seas that erode our coastlines, the gales that destroy cities and forests, the raging forest fires of over-dry summers, or the earthquakes and volcanoes that threaten to engulf some of our land. Climatic change, global warming, environmental conferences, CFC gases; our newspapers are full of such phrases. Nature is like our mother. We can abuse her and she will tolerate us because we are her children; but there will come a point when she has had enough. The Great Mother gives birth to our species, but she also receives us into death.

Unless we reconnect with Nature and come back into harmonious relationship with the other species around us, humankind will be rejected in the laboratory of the universe. In Wicca, humankind is seen not as a superior form of creation but as a species amongst others. All creation is our kin. Kinship

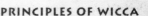

implies empathy both with the animal and with the plant kingdoms. Empathy implies mutual respect. Animal rights are important in Wicca and about half the Wiccan community are vegetarians. Ecology is another important issue. Many Witches belong to environmental groups and eco-magic to protect the planet is the main focus of some covens' activity. In this, Wicca is not alone. All over the world, indigenous traditions and tribal peoples are working towards the same ends.

In many Pagan cultures, we find the myth of a Golden Age when human beings and Nature dwelled in harmony. The Roman poet Ovid wrote in his *Metamorphoses* of the *Golden Age*.

Earth was untroubled,
unharried by hoe or ploughshare,
and brought forth all we needed.
And we were happy;
gathering berries from the mountain sides –
cherries, black caps, and edible acorns.
Spring was forever,
with a west wind blowing softly across the wild flowers.
The unploughed Earth brought forth rich grain.
The unfarrowed field whitened with wheat.
There were rivers of milk and rivers of honey,
and golden nectar dripped from the deep-green oaks.[2]

This may have been a vision of the future rather than a memory of the past; the hope of how our ancestors would have liked things to be, rather than the reality. However, regardless of the literal truth of such myths, they express something deep within the human psyche – a desire for oneness and harmony with the world around us. By celebrating Nature's cycle of change, we can attune ourselves once more to the natural world. We become part of the greater whole that is the universe itself.

Wicca has eight major festivals. These start at sunset and last to sunset the next day. Four are *solar* festivals whose timing is determined by the relationship of the Sun to the Earth. These are the Winter Solstice or Yule (the shortest day), Summer Solstice or Midsummer (the longest day), and the Spring and Autumn Equinoxes when the hours of darkness and light are equal. In the northern hemisphere, Yule is around December 21/22, Midsummer around June 21/22, Spring Equinox around March 20/21 and Autumn Equinox around September 21/22. I say 'around' because due to various idiosyncrasies of the Earth's orbit, the solstices and equinoxes can occasionally fall a day before or after the days I have given. In the southern hemisphere, in Australia for instance, the seasons are reversed. The Winter Solstice is on June 21.

The four other Wiccan festivals are Celtic in origin. These are Imbolc, absorbed into the Christian calendar as Candlemas – February 1/2; Beltane or May Eve on April 30/May 1; Lughnasadh also known by its Anglo-Saxon name of Lammas or Loaf Mass, July 31/August 1 and Samhain (pronounced sow-in) also known as All Hallow's Eve, October 31/November 1.

Ideally Witches celebrate their festivals on the correct date, but there is flexibility here. If the correct day is impractical we can have our celebration as near the date as possible.

Yule

Samhain/
Hallowe'en

Imbolc/
Candlemas

Autumn
Equinox

Spring
Equinox

Lughnasadh/
Lammas

Beltane/
May Eve

Midsummer

The Year's Wheel

Here is a brief description of some of the themes we can celebrate in the seasonal festivals. If you live in a temperate climate, whether north or south of the equator, then the sabbat cycle described here will be meaningful for you. If you live in hotter or colder climes, or regions of the world which do not have four distinct seasons, you will need to look at your own folk customs and traditions to discover the traditional festivals, when should they be celebrated, and how can you make a seasonal cycle that is meaningful for you. However, wherever you live, you will find the same themes of conception, birth, mating, maturation, death, rebirth, hidden beneath the surface of your folk traditions. These are cosmic and human realities and it is these which are at the root of our Wiccan traditions.

Imbolc Books about Wicca often describe Samhain as being the beginning of the Wiccan year. This idea originates in Irish Celtic tradition and works well when talking about the journey of the God as I do in Chapter 6. However, it was not part of

British Witchcraft until relatively recently. For most people, it is easier to think of the year starting with the awakening of the life force. In the temperate parts of the northern hemisphere, this means *Imbolc* or Candlemas when the first green shoots of bulbs appear; sometimes, as with snowdrops, coming up through the snow itself. This is a hopeful time. Life is stirring again. The forces of creativity are beginning to awaken.

The days grow noticeably longer. We know now that even if difficult times are still to come, hope is abroad in the land. In parts of the world where sheep are farmed, new lambs are born. One source of the Gaelic word *Imbolc* or *Oi-melc* is ewe's milk. Another idea is that the word means 'in the belly'. Traditional English Witches still call this festival by its name in the Christian calendar – *Candlemas*, the feast of candles. The Christian festival celebrates the *Purification of Virgin Mary*. The idea was that childbirth was polluting and women were not allowed into churches until they had undergone a purification ceremony. This is very different from Wicca where childbirth is a holy act. However, it does reflect an inherently Pagan idea – that this festival is about the Virgin Goddess.

What does this mean? Think of the power of Nature and of all green and growing things as the Goddess. With the onset of Autumn, the green vegetation disappears beneath the Earth. Symbolically we say, 'The Goddess is in the Underworld'. With Imbolc and the first signs of Nature's return, we say that the Goddess is returning to the land.

Magically, Imbolc is a good time to plan new enterprises and to make the first moves towards bringing them into actuality. Candle magic and magic for new beginnings are traditional at this time. However, it is best to proceed cautiously. It is time to design and plan, to dig foundations rather than to build. Imbolc is the first glimmering of the year's increase, but only the first glimmering. Frosts and snows may still come and nip

new life in the bud. In North America, February 2 is Ground Hog Day. This was unfamiliar to us in Europe until the film of the same name was released. A ground hog is a rodent and if it can see its shadow, then there is still much long cold winter to come.

Spring Equinox is the turning of the year, the point when light overcomes darkness. The hours of daylight grow longer than the hours of night. Lengthening days bring new growth. The sap rises in the tree. The sexual urge awakens in the animal world and in our own. Spring is the season of daffodils – blazes of golden yellow signal that the Sun grows stronger. Where we live in Brittany, in the north-west Celtic corner of France, along the roof ridges of the older thatched houses, people plant daffodils which come out around Spring Equinox. It looks rather crazy – all these little houses with daffodils growing out of their heads, but it's a true sign that Spring has come.

A more delicate flower for Spring is the primrose. This is best not picked; it withers too quickly. Pots can be sown with primrose seeds earlier in the year however and brought into the house to flower at Spring Equinox. They have the most beautiful and gentle light yellow colour. Customs from Spring have been woven into the Christian festival of Easter.

Spring Equinox celebrates the fertility of the land. It is a time to sow seeds both literally, in the sense of gardening or farming, and symbolically. Often seeds are sown at Spring Equinox which are imbued with magical intents. This is a piece of sympathetic magic that requires us to carefully nurture the seeds. You can see on a psychological level as well as on a magical one how the watering, potting out and protection of young seedlings is a constant reminder of the magical wish that we have made with their planting.

One of our students told us that where her father came from in Eastern England, there was a tradition that parsley should be sown on the first Friday of Spring by a blind man. Her father, not knowing a blind man, did this himself wearing a blindfold. Here we have a magical truth. Throughout our lives, our deeds and actions are sowing seeds. We do not see where they fall or how they will grow, but grow they will.

Spring Equinox in the northern hemisphere is when the Sun goes into the Astrological sign of Aries. Aries is a Fire sign. Impetuous Ariens leap in feet first and then wonder how they got there. The urge of Spring is to do, create, change, to get rid of the old and bring in the new – hence the old tradition of Spring cleaning the house. This is a valuable energy and we need it in our lives, but we also need to treat it with caution, balance and common sense.

Beltane is another word derived from Gaelic. It means 'bright fire'. In Ireland, bonfires were lit and cattle driven through the smoke and flames to rid their hides of parasites that had snuggled there through the cold winter. To leap the bonfire was to take the flame inside yourself. The flame of light, life and sun would bring new life; so even today Wiccan couples who want to conceive will leap the Beltane fire. With the stimulation of the pituitary gland by longer days and sunshine, sexuality is also stimulated – as of course Nature intended.

A heavily pregnant woman cannot till the land and just after giving birth is not an ideal time either. To bear children during the winter months after a well-fed spring and summer, when there was little to do but keep indoors and stay warm, was not such a bad idea. If a woman was not already pregnant by Beltane, this was a time for fertility magic. May Day ceremonies included men and women dancing together around phallic may-poles with women garlanded in flowers and strong ale flowing. If that did not help, some other May Eve customs might. Puritans in seventeenth century England wrote disapprovingly of how many virgins who went in the

woods to gather May Eve blossoms did not come out that way the next morning.

In European folklore traditions, the God appears at May Day in the guise of Jack-in-the-Green or the Green Man, the consort of the May Queen. In English country customs, the Green Man was disguised by his garment of leaves and in the freedom of anonymity could do what he willed. Similar customs are found in Germany and Austria in the form of masked celebrations which take place a little earlier in the year. This might also have solved some couples' fertility problems.

Hawthorn blossom, also known as May blossom, may be brought into the house to decorate it at Beltane. There are many superstitions about May blossom. Only Witches could bring it into the house with impunity, my mother told me, and let me bring it in. In Germany, where everything happens a little later than in Britain and Ireland's Gulf Stream climate, children make crowns of dandelions on May Day. For a few hours any-way, they really do look like angelic rays of sun.

Summer Solstice, the Longest Day, is the season of oak leaves and roses, symbols of God and of Goddess. Although both God and Goddess are present at Beltane and Midsummer, Beltane seems much more a Goddess festival; whereas Midsummer celebrates the God. In North America, Mother's Day falls in May near Beltane and Father's Day is near Midsummer. It seems to make sense to celebrate motherhood before fatherhood. It can take men a bit longer to become used to the idea.

Midsummer rites are often dedicated to the crowning of the solar king and the dedication of his male energy to the service of the Goddess, her people and her land. Paradoxically, this time is both the height of the sun and the beginning of its decline. After the peak there is nowhere to go but down.

This is a time when grass is cut for hay and the beautiful meadow smell of cut grass is everywhere. A natural instinct is to get up and watch the dawn on Midsummer Day and to celebrate the Sun in its fullness before its decline. Midsummer is a good time for men to do magic to help them in their everyday lives and for both sexes to do magic to help them with worldly matters – careers, houses, money. These are all the worldly but essential things we need for our material existence.

Lughnasadh is the Irish word for the August Eve festival and means the Games of Lugh. Lugh the God of Light instituted these games in honour of his mother-in-law which may be a poetic metaphor for the Mother Goddess. The alternative name, *Lammas*, is a Saxon word which means Loaf Mass. At Loaf Mass, the first loaf of bread was baked with the new wheat of the year.

What seems on the surface a simple thing – an ear of wheat – has many powerful connotations. Human invention of agriculture, like that of fire, was one of the great stepping stones in the advance of civilization. Once we learned to cultivate crops, our lives became much easier. We did not have to spend so much time searching for food than when we were hunter-gatherers relying on meat, fish, wild roots, leaves, berries and nuts for our sustenance.

In the Eleusinian Mysteries of ancient Greece, an ear of wheat was shown to the initiate as the final revelation. What did this mean? Try going out into the countryside at this time and picking an ear of wheat. Hold it in your hand and meditate upon it. What does it tell you? How does it feel? The ripened ear of wheat has not the smoothness of youth, but the ripeness of age. It is dry, but has the promise of transformation. New life can spring from it; for within it is the seed. Within the seed is the promise of reincarnation and rebirth. This was the secret revealed to the initiate: we are born, live, die and live again.

Another message of Lammas is sacrifice. In ancient times in some societies, the king was considered Divine. He must die at

the peak of his powers so that his strength and energy might pass to the new king. There is a message here for us all and it is about facing up to change. Middle age and death are part of life's realities. We must accept that, whatever our worldly achievements, at some point we are going to have to let them go. We will have to take a step forward into the unknown – the realm of death and the after-life. This involves an inner sacrifice; letting go of all that we have gained in life and detaching ourselves from the past.

Lammas magic can be magic of detachment. It is a time to let go of past griefs, hates, angers and injustices and to move forward. This is a good time for divorce. It is also, paradoxically, a goodtime for marriage for people who intend being spiritual partners as well as intending to have children or to pursue material lives together. This is not a good time for founding material enterprises: Imbolc is a better time to lay foundation stones. However, Lammas can be a good time to found spiritual enterprises.

Autumn Equinox At Lammas the corn king is killed and disappears on the material plane but does not go away completely. He is preparing to enter the spiritual realm. Spiritual enterprises founded at Lammas will not manifest until Autumn Equinox, which is when the tide turns again from the outer world to the inner.

Autumn is the season of the apple harvest and of hops and grapes. In warmer climates it is the time of Dionysus, the God of Wine. Autumn Equinox is a celebration but also an ending of summer and a preparation for the cold to come. Autumn is the time when stags begin their rutting and challenge one another across forest clearings. Battles are fought and won, with the stronger stag claiming the hinds as his right. His unsuccessful rivals will be marginalized, left to graze on the edge of the herd to await their chance another year.

Our modern practice of starting the school year at autumn is a sensible one. Autumn magic is magic of the mind. It is time to start studying as the nights draw in and the outside world is less of a distraction. As the night-time world comes to dominate the year, it is also a time to develop our magical and psychic powers. The first half of the year, the morning of the year, is about the outer world. The second half or evening of the year is about the inner world and spiritual realm.

One simple way of celebrating Autumn is to float a candle down a flowing river as a sign that the sun is going away from us for a time. In many cultures we find the idea of floating candles on streams, rivers or the sea as part of autumn seasonal rites. It is a natural thing for humans to do – to create the meeting of the elements is always magical. At this time, we celebrate the descent of the Goddess to the underworld.

Samhain is Irish for 'Summer's end'. Whereas in most of northern Europe, summer seems to end with Autumn Equinox, winter comes later to Ireland and to other western parts of Europe warmed by the Gulf stream. Leaves are on the trees for much longer and the traditional planting season for trees does not start until early November.

Samhain is the festival of the dead in Pagan custom. Modern society does everything it can to separate us from death. My father remembered seeing dead bodies from an early age. It was the custom in his part of Ireland to hold a wake – a party to celebrate someone who had died. The dead person was an honoured guest – laid out in an open coffin or, in some cases, propped up in the corner in his or her favourite chair. In Brittany until the 1950s, in traditional villages, bodies were buried under the church floors, dug up again once the flesh had fallen from the bones, and then the bones and skulls were displayed in ossuaries at the entrance to the church. You could stop on the way into church and say a quick prayer in front of Granny's

thigh bone. These are the same customs that our Neolithic ancestors followed 5,000–8,000 years ago. Death and the dead were constantly present and were treated with less fear.

Today, many of us have little contact with the generations that preceded us, but a sense of who we are and where we have come from is important to us all. It is also important to honour the past and those human beings whose genes have made us what we are. Their hopes, fears, joys, sorrows, triumphs and despairs are woven into the fabric of our psyches, though below the threshold of consciousness.

One way of celebrating Samhain is to build an altar to our ancestors and to find old photographs, mementos, medals, and to put them in a place of honour for the festival. We not only have physical ancestors, we also have spiritual ancestors; those whose dreams and visions have created the Wiccan spiritual life that we have today. For Samhain, why not do some research into the great and good, or the great and not-always-so-good, of our Pagan past? Other religious traditions have their saints and great teachers. Let us honour those who have given us the knowledge from the past that now takes us forward into the future.

Winter Solstice is the low point of the year in terms of daylight and energy. In our centrally heated houses with enough food to eat all year, it is difficult for us to understand the dangers and perils of winter. The winter season is still when many older people die, struck down by illness, and this was even more the case for our ancestors. Grain had to be stored from the summer's harvest and most animals had to be killed as there was insufficient grazing to keep them through the winter. There was always the real danger that if winter was long, food might run out.

With Winter Solstice, the wheel of the year reaches its lowest point and shortest day, and then – the great miracle – the day grows just marginally longer. In symbolic language we say:

The Goddess has given birth to the reborn Sun.
She has brought forth the Child of Promise.
There is hope again in the land.
The wheel has turned.

Winter Solstice or Yule was a time for feasting. It was a time to enjoy goose or pig; to decorate the house with greenery and bright red-berried holly; to burn one of the biggest logs in a great warm blaze; to bake sweet honeyed cakes, to buy treats for the children from passing pedlars – brightly coloured ribbons, a wooden toy. All these were ways to affirm hope in the dark time and to bring just a little colour and joy into winter's hardships and cold.

In the next two chapters, we explore magic in Wicca, but before going any further, here are some ideas for beginning to celebrate the cycle of the season's change.

Festival	Altar Decorations	Colour	Magic
Imbolc	Snowdrops and other late winter bulbs, candles	White, pale green	Cleansing, healing, purity, candle magic
Spring Equinox	Spring flowers, painted green eggs, catkins, seed cake	Green	Seed planting, fertility magic, magic to begin new enterprises and worldly activities
Beltane	Hawthorn and other blossom, ribbons, flowery crowns, decorated poles	Green, white and pink	Sex magic, fertility magic

Festival	Altar Decorations	Colour	Magic
Midsummer	Roses, oak leaves, symbols of the Sun	Yellow, red, green	Magic for men and for worldly affairs
Lughnasadh, Lammas	Newly cut wheat, corn dollies, fresh baked bread, sickles	Orange	Letting go, spiritual marriage, priesthood, divorce
Autumn Equinox	Apples, fallen leaves, pine cones, antlers	Orange, brown, gold, red	Magic to increase intellectual, psychic-spiritual powers weaving magic
Samhain	Apples, spirals, branches of dead leaves, black mirrors, crystal balls, cauldrons	Brown, black	Divination
Yule	An evergreen tree (preferably one which can be replanted), anything reminiscent of the Sun – golden apples, holly and mistletoe, sparkling crystals, candles, a hearth fire	Black, gold, white, red, green	Celebration, magic for children's health or to conceive

Sabbat Correspondences

CELEBRATING THE SEASONAL CYCLE – COMMUNING WITH NATURE

If we want to celebrate the seasonal cycle, how can we begin? The sabbats celebrate the changing face of Nature. To begin to understand them, we must go outside to see what is happening. As near as you can to the sabbat date, go for a walk, ideally in the countryside, or if not in a city park. Look at what is going on in Nature around you. Are the trees budding, in blossom, in full leaf, fruiting, covered with dead leaves or bare? What are the birds doing, the animals, the flowers?

Time spent with nature can be healing. Life in polluted cities where we cannot see the horizon is unnatural for an animal such as humankind and is stressful. When rats live in overcrowded conditions, they attack one another. When humans are overcrowded we get neighbourhood violence and road rage. The need for solitude, silence and greenness is strongly advocated in Wicca. In the United States the great nineteenth-century thinker Ralph Waldo Emerson wrote:

> In the woods ... a man casts off his years as the snake his slough, and at what period soever of life is always a child. In the woods is perpetual youth. Within these plantations of God a decorum and sanctity reign, a perennial festival is dressed, and the guest sees not how he should tire of them in a thousand years. In the woods we return to reason and faith. There I feel that nothing can befall me in life – no disgrace, no calamity (leaving me my eyes), which nature cannot repair. Standing on the bare ground – my head bathed by the blithe air, and uplifted into infinite space – all mean egoism banishes. I become a transparent eye-ball; I am nothing: I see all; the currents of the Universal Being circulate through me: I am part or particle of God.[3]

Whilst a Witch might say, 'Goddess', these sentiments are still true today. One of the traditional images of the Witch is of the old Wise Woman, who lives alone in a clearing in the middle of the wood, with only her familiars – owl, crow, cat, bat, frog, toad, snake – for company. To be alone with Nature; to listen to the noises of the wood; to have times of silence, solitude and peace; all this enables us to hear the inner voices of the Gods and to learn their will. It gives us time to reflect on our daily life and how we can live it more wisely and well.

CREATING A SEASONAL ALTAR

An altar is a focal point for worship and for veneration of the Divine powers of the universe. Why, might you ask, do we need an altar when the Divine is all around us? Our minds are lazy. An altar helps draw our attention to the Divine reality that lies behind our everyday world. Making an altar reminds us of the sacred and of our relation to it.

An altar can be anywhere. It need not be obtrusive. You can make an altar simply by placing symbols of the four elements on a shelf, table or desk in your home or workplace, or in your garden. People might think your taste in decor is a little eccentric, but only you and magically-minded friends will notice that you have symbolized the four elements. Creating an altar can be a meditative and devotional act in itself. In so-called primitive societies, people spend hours of their time creating something beautiful and sometimes ephemeral for ritual, like body painting, just to please themselves, one another and the Gods.

1. Decide where to create your altar. Usually Wiccan altars are in the north of a room, or in the centre with their backs to the north. Observe the movements of the Sun or use a compass to work out the position of north. You may then find that a northern altar would not be practical and will need to put it

in another direction. This does not matter, but if later you come to create ritual, you may prefer to orient your altar to the north.

2. You can use a small table, a shelf or a chest for your altar. This may be attractive enough in itself. If not, you may want to cover it with a piece of cloth appropriate to the season.

3. You will need something to represent each of the four elements: candles for Fire; incense, a feather or bell for Air; a bowl of water for Water; and a bowl of earth or a rock for Earth.

4. Now you have the beginnings of your altar, you need appropriate seasonal decorations. Have a look at Figure 3 for some ideas. Go for a walk and try to find some seasonal flowers or greenery to bring home for your altar.

5. Once you have made your altar, take some time to meditate in front of it. Festivals begin at sunset, so this is a good time to begin, but if this is not practical then you can begin your meditation at any time.

6. First light a candle and some incense if you have it. Think about the themes of the festival. How might they apply to your life? Ask the Gods to assist you with any problems that you may have at this time. Take a small piece of plain card or paper and write down your problems and requests and leave it hidden somewhere on or under the altar where no one can see. When it is time to change your altar for the next season, read it to see if there have been any changes in your situation and then burn your requests in a candle flame. Maybe the Gods will have heard you, maybe not; but it is important to ask, to articulate our need. The universe does listen, even if our requests cannot be answered exactly how and when we wish.

7. Communing with Nature and making a seasonal altar are ways of beginning to celebrate the sabbats. Later you might want to create some sabbat rituals. I talk about this in Chapter 8.

PRINCIPLES OF WICCA

48   Notes

1. Kenneth Hurlstone Jackson, *A Celtic Miscellany*, Penguin, Harmondsworth 1971, pages 66–7.
2. Quoted in C Merchant, *The Death of Nature: Woman, Ecology and the Scientific Revolution*, Wildwood House, London 1982, page 31.
3. Ralph Waldo Emerson, 'Nature', in *Selected Essays*, Penguin, Harmondsworth 1983 ed, pages 38–9.

THE MAGICAL REALM

Some people are more attracted to the Nature religion side of Wicca, others to its magic-making, others to a combination of these. But what is magic?

Magic is causing change by means not yet accepted by science. This does not mean that magic and science will not eventually meet, but that science is still struggling to catch up. It is important that we are not blinded by science. Science is the sum of accepted human knowledge at a certain time – and the boundaries are always moving. Usually, any new leap in scientific thinking is ridiculed by the majority of scientists. It only becomes accepted after long and heated debate in scientific journals. Many ideas that were common in magic and mysticism were dismissed by eighteenth- and nineteenth-century science, only to be embraced again by twentieth-century quantum physics and chaos theory.

There are two types of magic – *natural magic* and *high magic* (sometimes spelled *magick*). We use high magic to transform ourselves into more evolved human beings. In Wicca, high magic involves initiatory rites and rites of worship which put us in touch with the Divine within and without. Over time, if these rites are performed well, they make permanent changes in our inner being and state of consciousness. The ends are the same as those of all the mystical traditions and of more evolved forms of spiritual psychology. The means may differ in that Wicca, like ritual magic, uses rites and ceremonies. Rites of worship are described in Chapter 8 and the initiatory aspect of Wicca in Chapter 9.

NATURAL MAGIC

Natural magic seeks to cause changes on the material plane rather than inner changes. It involves using the properties of external things such as crystals and metals, herbs, planetary and lunar influences; harnessing their energies and flowing with their tides. Magic can also involve the agency of third parties – angels, spirits, elementals, but this is not so common in Wicca as in some forms of ritual magic. Wicca tends to rely on the innate knowledge and abilities of the Witch – the powers of the human mind. This knowledge was the province of Wise Women and Cunning Men, the original healers, midwives and horse doctors, who are sometimes now known by Rae Beth's beautiful but modern term *Hedgewitch*.[1]

Much of the learning and lore of the village Wise Woman and Cunning Man has passed into modern science. Herbalism was incorporated into modern medicine. Willow bark gave way to aspirin. Modern chemistry synthesized chemical versions of herbal medicine in scientific laboratories; but in some cases the original has been found to be better. Weather magic became meteorology and weather forecasting; but individual practitioners who rely on traditional systems, such as reading sunspots, often do better than national weather laboratories – and make a good commercial living out of doing so. Other knowledge was neglected because it did not fit in with the scientific paradigms of the time. It was a long time before medicine accepted that emotional trauma could cause serious physical illness and that cure could come about only by tackling the emotional as well as the physical problems. Any traditional healer could have told us – if only he or she had been asked. The reason why science could not encompass these ideas was because of limitations in its world view.

Western society during the past two to three hundred years has embraced the rational. The awakening of rationality was necessary to develop our intellectual faculties and to rescue us from the stranglehold of superstition. At the same time it led to a denial of the spiritual realm.

With the rise of rationalism, the idea that spiritual forces influence our lives and destinies; that Nature is ensouled; that as well as a physical body we have a spiritual centre which can communicate in non-physical ways with the spiritual centres of others; all this was rejected. We lost our ability to be in touch with past and future through clairvoyance; to sense subtle energies around us, and to use our energy for magical purposes. All these thoughts, ideas and dreams were shut away in the cellar of the unconscious.

CLAIRVOYANCE

Wicca today works with and develops those powers that sometimes go by the name of *parapsychology*. These are the powers of telepathy – knowing what someone else who is not present is thinking or feeling; clairvoyance – obtaining information about the future, often in the form of pictures rather than words; psychometry – finding information about things by touching them; dowsing – using a pendulum or divining rod to locate things; and psychokinesis – causing physical change through the use of the mind. The latter is often called magic and the former skills are lumped together under the heading of divination.

Some people seek deliberately to cultivate these powers. Dowsing is an example. It is used by practical people such as farmers to locate underground sources of water to dig for wells, by archaeologists seeking to find ancient buildings, by oil explorers and in some cases by the police seeking corpses in murder cases. People may also use the tarot or other divinatory systems to tap into their clairvoyance. Many of us also have spontaneous parapsychological experiences, such as premonitions of death or disaster; seeing ghosts; sensing that a house has a bad atmosphere and finding that a tragedy has occurred there. Most of us have had less dramatic experiences such as dreaming of an old friend and bumping into them the next day in an unexpected place. All these are common occurrences.

Magic involves the active use and projection of our inner powers. Clairvoyance is in some ways just the opposite. It is about learning to be still, passive and receptive. Clairvoyants are those who by birth or training are more able than the rest of us to notice subtle signals. As human beings, we are bombarded with information. Some information is visual. Other information comes via ears, tongue, skin, nose; in other words through the five senses. We also receive information through what is sometimes called the *sixth sense*. We know, but we do not know how we know: we simply know. Wicca seeks to develop and fine tune this sixth sense. The information perceived by the sixth sense is like a weak signal that is competing with much stronger ones from the traditional five senses. We are not trained to notice it, so it becomes lost.

Part of Wiccan training is to become more aware of the 'weak' signals. These signals are stronger when we are relaxed, meditating or dreaming. If you pick up any good text on magic, it will tell you to begin by recording your dreams. Much of what goes through our minds when we are dreaming involves processing events that have happened in our everyday lives.

Other information comes from deeper levels of consciousness.

The idea that dreams foretell the future is an age-old one. The Pagan temples of the ancient world had special incubation rooms where people with difficult problems would sleep to ask the Gods to send them the answer to their problem. Sometimes a trained priest or priestess would do it on the individual's behalf. If we start to record our dreams immediately on waking, we will find that we will gradually remember more and more. 'Immediately' does mean immediately. We must have pen and paper by the bed and start writing as soon as we wake up, before the dream memory disappears. If we record our dreams over a period of, say, a month, we may find a number of interesting things. One is that when we dream we often see our friends, relatives, colleagues and partners in a different way from when we are awake. We will find that all sorts of hidden conflicts, tensions and jealousies reveal themselves to us in dreams of which we were unaware.

This is not clairvoyance but it is similar in that we are noticing the 'weak signals'; thoughts that are unconscious or repressed. We will also find other information in our dreams – premonitions of the future. Most of us have heard of spectacular dreams of the future: people whose lives are saved because they dream their holiday plane will crash and decide not to take the trip. Usually, however, clairvoyance is much more mundane than this.

By learning to remember our dreams, we become more open to other messages from the unconscious in our waking life. These are the premonitions, dreams and hunches which people experience but often ignore. How often have we 'known' not to take a particular route to work today because the traffic will be bad – and have ignored it only to find ourselves fuming in a traffic jam? How often have we had a 'bad feeling' about someone and have become involved with them only to regret it?

Perhaps we have taken a job with misgivings only to find that there was something unexpectedly disastrous – the firm goes bust or we find ourselves working with impossible colleagues. Not all our hunches are accurate. Sometimes they reflect our fears and inadequacies but they are extra information in any situation which must be checked. There is nothing more irrational than to override what our feelings tell us and to rely entirely on logic.

Some aspects of clairvoyance rely not just on innate psychic abilities but on complex philosophical systems. These include astrology and geomancy, the science of reading earth energies, which in Chinese is called *Feng Shui*. In the economically booming Far East, whole business empires are guided by astrologers who help read trends in the financial markets. Once at a scientific conference, astrology was being mocked when a famous British businesswoman asked a panel of scientists, 'But how do you know when not to write a business letter if you don't know when Mercury is in retrograde?' There were howls of laughter from the scientists but they failed to notice an important fact: the businesswoman earned four times more than they did.

WHO CAN DO MAGIC?

In most traditional societies, Witchcraft was the prerogative of a trained professional – Shaman, Medicine Man, Medicine Woman, Witch Doctor, Cunning Man, Wise Woman, Witch. These professional practitioners often inherited their 'businesses' from a mother or father. In some societies, they were people who had undergone a special spiritual crisis. They were chosen by the Gods and set apart. Their paths were for the chosen few and were not always thought desirable callings. Most people do not want to be set apart from their fellows by strangeness or by the ability to enter other worlds.

Traditional Witches often hold the view that Witches are born, not made. A contrasting attitude was that of magician Aleister Crowley. 'Magick is for all,' he wrote at the beginning of the twentieth century, 'the Banker, the Pugilist, the Biologist, the Poet, the Navvy, the Grocer, the Factory Girl, the Mathematician, the Stenographer, the Golfer, the Wife, the Consul – and all the rest – to fulfil themselves perfectly, each in his or her own proper function.'[2] In modern times, attitudes amongst Witches have changed. This is why old Craft teachers started to bring outsiders into their traditions; not to be 'professional Witches' but to learn to integrate the magical arts into their everyday lives.

People often come into Wicca saying, 'I'd like to be a Witch but I don't know if I'd be any good at magic.' Most Witches are better at some aspects of Wicca than others. It may be creating high magic ritual; it may be spellcraft or divination; it may be herb lore; it may be a deep spiritual love of the Gods. However, we can all develop some magical skills.

Many books about magic suggest that you must believe before you practise. This is not my experience. Magic can be approached in the same way as anything from acupuncture to riding a bicycle. Try it and see if it works. What is important is not unshakeable belief, but open-mindedness. If we decide we cannot do something or it will not work, then of course it will not. We will set up a resistance. It is a bit like fire-walking. Providing we do it calmly and without fear, we will not burn ourselves. If we panic or do not believe in ourselves, we may fail.

Self-belief is an important aspect of Wicca. This does not mean we have to believe we are the greatest Witches in the universe. It does mean that we must believe it is permissible for nice things to happen to us. In our unstable society, many people have family backgrounds that leave them with feelings of

low self-esteem. They feel unloved, unworthy and deserving only the worst. If we have these negative attitudes, then it is difficult to believe that our own magical energy can change our lives. To begin to feel empowered, we must start making small improvements in our lives. Having the will to do even the smallest thing to make our lives better will give us self-confidence and self-belief. Decorate a room that has always been drab. Go through your wardrobe and throw away all the clothes that you never wear and which you know do not suit you. Wash the car, tidy the house, give yourself a treat – not a chocolate doughnut but something worthwhile – a trip to the countryside, a day off. Plant something beautiful, have a massage, go for a swim; anything that gives you enjoyment and is good for you. This may seem a strange way to begin magic, but these simple actions are ways of sending messages to our unconscious minds that we are worthy people, worthy of love. We can then allow magic to enter our lives.

Our attitude to magic must be similar to that required for spiritual healing. 'Faith' healing requires that the patient believes in the healer and his or her world view, religion, system, etc. Spiritual healing needs only that the patient be open to something happening. Interestingly, people often prefer to believe that nothing is happening, even when it is. In my spiritual healing practice, I have treated many a reluctant husband dragged along by his wife who was fed up of his complaints about a chronic illness. Having sat with gritted teeth for half an hour, swearing that nothing was happening, the husband would disappear, only to reappear again the next week for a follow-up session – this time alone. When asked if there had been any improvement, I would get a reluctant, 'Well, a bit.' It was always, 'Well a bit', until they stopped coming because they were cured.

Many objects used in magic have no inherent value of their own but can carry a 'charge' of our energy and serve as props to aid concentration. Traditional objects include cords, where the knotting action is used as a focus for the magical intent; candles – the flame is used to aid concentration; wax images – these often receive negative press and people think of them as something to stick pins into but we use them for healing. These are useful props but what is more important are the internal processes that go on within the Witch. Four important things are:

visualization
changed states of consciousness (trance)
concentration
etheric energy.

VISUALIZATION

Magic works using visual images. The meadow exercise that I asked you to try at the end of Chapter 2 is a visualization exercise. If you are someone with a vivid imagination, you will have found the exercise easy. If not you will need to practise. Try sitting on your bed and looking around your room. Close your eyes and visualize just one part of the room and the objects in it. Open your eyes and check how well you have done. You will probably find that you have missed out a lot. Practise this technique whenever you have some spare time – sitting on a bus, waiting for an appointment, during a boring meeting.

If you find visualization difficult, most large cities have classes in visualization techniques. These are used in many fields from healing to psychotherapy to art to sport. Initially visualization is easier in a group. Visual images are much

easier to create if a number of people are visualizing the same thing at the same time.

CONCENTRATION

Magic and visualizations such as the meadow exercise require concentration. This can be difficult, particularly if we have busy lives and find it difficult to 'switch off'. Do not worry too much about your mind wandering at first. If you notice your mind has wandered off, pull it gently back. It is a bit like riding a horse that wants to wander off the track. Give the reins a tug and get it back on course.

TRANCE

Trance involves moving into an altered state of consciousness and entering a timeless zone. This need not involve losing awareness of everyday reality; but the focus of attention is elsewhere – resting lightly in the centre of oneself; floating tranquilly on the sea of one's own consciousness. Things that can induce relaxation such as incense, candle light, firelight, soft music, chakra exercises, chanting, dance and drumming will help us enter a trance state. These are the psychotechnology of all spiritual and magical traditions.

Trance involves a change of brain state. In our normal state a fast pattern of activity known as *Beta* predominates. This helps us focus on the present. This is a very useful state of being. When we are crossing a busy street we do not want to be bombarded by clairvoyant messages.

We achieve a deeper state of consciousness when much slower *Theta* waves predominate. Here we are aware not just of the present, but of past and future. The boundaries of individual psyches become permeable and 'leakage' occurs from one person to another. We most often enter Theta consciousness when we are in the dreaming stage of sleep. This is when most people receive psychic messages, but those who do not remember their dreams are liable to lose them. Magic requires us to achieve Theta consciousness when we are awake. This must be handled carefully. Some meditation systems cause individuals to have sudden 'openings'. This is not a good idea. Opening the psyche too quickly can cause psychological breakdown.

Between the Beta and Theta patterns in terms of speed of brain activity is another pattern – *Alpha*. We tend to enter this state when we relax with our eyes closed. Alpha consciousness is a gateway to the deeper states of consciousness that we need to develop for magic. Some people are born with the gift of entering these deeper states of consciousness. These are the natural Witches, Yogis and mystics. Others must learn to achieve them. Many meditation techniques can help us. The exercise of opening our chakras which is described at the end of this chapter can also help.

ETHERIC ENERGY

Witches have always believed that the body has certain energies that can be directed, used or sent elsewhere to achieve a particular end. As well as a physical body, we also have an etheric body. This is an energy field which surrounds and **permeates** the physical body. The etheric body has special **energy** centres that in Sanskrit are called *Chakras* or wheels. These are points whereby the etheric body transmits and receives energy. It is this etheric energy that we see when we see people's auras. Etheric energy is stronger in the more spiritually and magically powerful. This is why great spiritual figures such as Buddha and the Christian saints were portrayed as having halos around their heads, or in Buddha's case, the thousand-petalled lotus.

The halo is really a depiction of the crown chakra around the top of the head. In the more advanced of us this is very active. These energy systems were known to our Celtic ancestors. The Druids knew of at least three of the centres. During the Christian era such knowledge was lost.

There are seven major chakras in the body. These are associated with different colours.

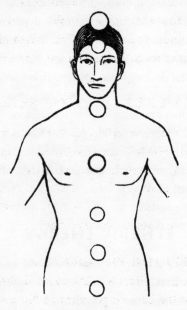

The Major Chakras

The base of spine chakra is red. It replenishes the physical energy of the body and is associated with the element of Earth. The sacral chakra is orange. It is associated with the sexual and urinary systems and the element of Water; also with raw, animalistic emotion. The solar plexus is golden yellow and is associated with love and healing. If you are in any of the healing or helping professions, you should ensure that your solar plexus

energy does not become depleted. The heart chakra is green. It
is associated with altruistic love and compassion, as opposed to
the more personal love of the solar plexus chakra. The heart
chakra can be strengthened by daily meditation. The throat
chakra is blue and is used in inspirational speaking. It is needed in occupations that involve teaching, communicating with
and guiding others. The third eye is associated with clairvoyance. Its colour is violet. If you shut your eyes in the daytime
you will probably find that you see violet if you focus on the
point midway between your brows. The crown chakra is our
link to the Divine and its colour is brilliant white light.

SIMPLE EXERCISES TO BEGIN

DEVELOPING MAGICAL ENERGIES –
CHAKRA EXERCISE

Opening our energy centres, the chakras, is helpful when we
are about to do magic. It will ensure that we have energy to
project and that we remember to replenish ourselves, so that
our own energy store does not become depleted.

OPENING THE CHAKRAS

1. To open the chakras, first visualize a round circle of pulsating red light at the base of your spine. Now imagine that
   you are drawing a current of energy into the chakra so that
   it grows warm and begins to glow and pulsate with red
   energy and light. Visualize the base of spine chakra growing larger until it covers the whole of your lower spine.
2. Draw more and more energy into the base of spine chakra.
   Then, as the flow of energy comes into your body, allow it
   to coil round and round inside you like a snake. Allow the
   snake of energy to rise, still spiralling, until it reaches the
   level of your belly.

3. Visualize the snake spiralling round and round at the level of your belly. As it does so, visualize your sacral chakra in the centre of your belly beginning to glow with spinning orange light. Allow the orange circle to grow larger and larger, spinning with energy.

4. Draw more energy up the spine and into the sacral chakra, so that this spins faster and grows wider, glowing with a bright orange light. Then allow the snake of energy to rise up through the centre of your body to the level of the solar plexus. Here it begins to activate the solar plexus chakra that starts to glow with a golden yellow light.

5. Go back down to the base of the spine and draw more energy up the centre of the body and into the solar plexus chakra. Allow it to open wider and wider. Allow the chakra to spin faster and faster until there is a golden spinning sun at the solar plexus.

6. Go back to the base of the spine again. Draw more energy in and up the spine, past the sacral chakra, past the solar plexus, up to the centre of the breast bone, where there is a small green fiery glow which is the heart chakra. Let the energy you have drawn upwards feed the fiery glow, so that it begins to spin faster and faster, and grow wider and wider, until it covers the whole of your chest with a green glowing light.

7. Go back to the base of the spine again and draw energy up through the spine, past the heart chakra to the throat, where there is a small blue glow. Allow the energy to stream into the throat and to spin the chakra faster and faster until there is a pulsating blue centre at the throat.

8. Go back to the base of the spine again to renew your energy. Draw energy in through the base of spine chakra, up through the sacral chakra, through the solar plexus, through the heart chakra, to the throat. Then go back to the

base of the spine again. Draw a current of energy right up through the body, up past the throat and into the third eye at the centre of the forehead. Allow this energy to merge with the violet spot at the third eye and to spin the third eye energy faster and faster until there is a spiralling violet centre in the middle of the forehead.

9. Go back to the base of the spine. Draw more energy into the body and up past the sacral chakra, past the solar plexus, past the heart, past the throat and into the third eye. Allow the violet glow to spin faster and faster. Then allow the current of energy to shoot up through the head and out of the crown. Allow the energy to cascade down your body, bathing it in light, and flowing down to your feet in a white stream.

10. Go back to the base of the spine. Draw up more energy right up through the body, past the sacral chakra, past the solar plexus, past the heart, past the throat, past the third eye and out again through the crown chakra and down the body to the feet. Repeat this a few times and then relax.

You may find some chakras more difficult to open than others. If you have problems with the sacral chakra, try opening the chakras in the reverse order – from the crown chakra down. There will be a build up of energy before you reach the sacral chakra which will make it easier to open. For those who have problems with the throat chakra, singing a few notes or sounds just before starting can help.

FEELING ETHERIC ENERGY

Once you have opened your chakras, this is a simple exercise you can do to help you become more aware of your etheric energy.

1. Open your chakras. Imagine the solar plexus chakra activating the whole area around the middle of your body and hence

flowing straight into your lower arms. There is an intimate connection between the solar plexus chakra and your hands, although this is not so obvious anatomically. Now allow energy from your solar plexus chakra to flow down your arms and into your hands. Visualize your hands beginning to glow with yellow light. If you find that channelling energy is draining, try going back to the base of the spine and drawing energy into yourself more frequently. This will stop you feeling depleted.

2. Now close your eyes and slowly bring the palms of your hands together until you can feel the energy from one hand pressing against the other. Open your eyes and see how far apart your hands were when you began to sense your energy. If you do this exercise over a period of time, you will find that your ability to project energy from hand to hand will grow steadily stronger.

CLOSING THE CHAKRAS

If we have opened the chakras, we must also close them. This can be done more quickly than opening them. One of the easiest ways is to imagine each chakra as a stained glass window of the appropriate colour.

1. Starting at the top, the crown chakra, draw a fountain of white light down the outside of your whole body. Let it flow over the third eye, closing the chakra completely as though a white shutter is being drawn over it.

2. Then draw more white light down from the crown past the third eye to the throat chakra, and then over the throat, shutting the chakra.

3. Draw more light from the crown down and over the heart chakra.

4. Now draw more white light down over the top of the head,

over the third eye, over the throat, over the heart chakra and down over the solar plexus chakra.

5. Then from the crown of the head draw more white light down past the solar plexus, past the sacral and down to the base of the spine.

6. Do not attempt to close the base of spine chakra or crown chakras. These are left open to absorb energy.

Some people find that they acquire a heightened awareness of their body through this exercise.

Notes

1. Rae Beth, *Hedgewitch*, Hale, London 1990.
2. Aleister Crowley, *Magick in Theory and Practice*, Castle Books, NY, page xi.

USING OUR MAGICAL ENERGIES

If we decide to try magic for ourselves, how do we go about it? At the end of this chapter is an exercise in candle magic. First, though, here are some ideas on how to make your magic work.

WHAT SHOULD WE USE MAGIC FOR?

Magic is a force, a power, a wisdom, a knowledge. It is both more and less powerful than the ignorant suppose. Magic can only change the changeable. It can cure a sickness; it cannot regrow a lost limb. In Wicca, magic is carried out according to strict ethics. For this reason, coven training takes a long time. Matches are not put into the hands of children, nor power into the hands of the untrained and untested. Magic is not a power we use in place of our other powers – mind, emotion, hand and limb. It is not a crutch for the weak, nor an ego-boost for the inadequate. It is a skill that we must learn to use wisely and well.

'Wisely and well' means in the right time and place, when other avenues on the material plane have been explored. Wicca teaches people sound ethical principles for the use of magic and encourages their spiritual development hand in hand with any powers that they wish to develop. This can be boring and frustrating to the would-be Witch who just wants to get on with it, but going through the boredom threshold is an aspect of any learning, be it playing a musical instrument or learning a language.

Most people do not come to Wicca seeking magical training in order to make a lot of money and gain power over others. There are much simpler ways of achieving this – become a lawyer or an accountant. The usual problem is not people wanting to do negative magic but the 'astral bandage syndrome': people wanting to use their new-found powers to put the world to rights. New Witches can easily become interfering nuisances, wanting to cure everyone of every illness, whether they want it or not.

Magic is a simple force but applying it skilfully is difficult. In seemingly simple situations, there can be many complex factors. Even if someone has asked for healing, there can be many barriers within the person that can prevent it. On one level, he or she may want to be well. On another level, the illness may be serving the individual in some way. It may bring attention to the neglected. It may be a way of hiding from a relationship, job or another aspect of life that someone finds untenable.

There is a traditional Witchcraft saying, 'If it harms none, do what you will.' Often there is long debate in covens about particular pieces of magical work. It is very important that if you are in a group you take time to check that everyone is happy with any piece of magic you are going to do. If people are half-hearted or have hidden resentments, firstly the magic is unlikely to work and secondly they will feel disempowered. When we enter into trance and do magic, there is not a total dissolving of the boundaries between ourselves and others, but there is a blurring of this distinction. To allow this to happen, we need to be able to love and trust those with whom we are working. This involves treating one another with mutual respect.

This is one of the reasons why traditionally covens are small, closed groups. To build bonds requires time and mutual knowledge. This cannot be achieved quickly; nor is it possible to have this type of loving relationship with everyone.

Some covens believe that you should not do magic for yourself and if someone in the group has requested help, he or she will not participate in the spell that gives it. In most covens, however, people can work for themselves providing the group thinks it is appropriate. There are a number of reasons why working for ourselves is not a good idea. One is the delusion of the ego and our own self-centredness. It is very easy for us to convince ourselves that what we want is right and appropriate. It takes long years of training for us to become objective about such things. This is one advantage of belonging to a group. If we take our problems to our group, they can be much more objective about them than we are and can advise us if it is appropriate to tackle them with magic or not.

Love is an important aspect of magic. This is not some New Age idea but a good Wiccan principle also found in modern psychology. The founder of the psychotherapeutic system of psychosynthesis, Italian psychologist Roberto Assagioli who had studied much esoteric teaching, wrote:

> We must realize that love, in order to truly fulfil its mission of being helpful ... must be allied to insight; even more, permeated and blended with wisdom; without understanding there cannot be harmlessness.[1]

The same is true of magic. We must combine it with common sense, worldly wisdom and spiritual insight if it is to do its work.

Magic is the power to change ourselves and to change society. For true magic we must want to reach out positively to something beyond the boundaries of the self. This emotion is love. Love operates on many different levels. There is the love of ourselves; the love of those close to us – parents, children, partners, siblings; the love for country and land; the love for humanity as a whole and the love for all creation – both the physical world of Nature and that which lies beyond – the realm of the Gods.

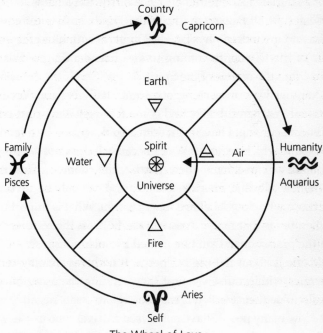

The Wheel of Love

If we talk about love of country, people can become nervous, but this need not mean unthinking patriotism. It is good to respect our own culture and people but the dangers of nationalism are all too present in the world today. Perhaps we need to think of ourselves more as citizens (and tenants) of the Earth itself; that it is terrestrial and not national boundaries that define us. Wicca is less anthropocentric than monotheisms. These tend to believe that the universe was created for the benefit of human beings.

This is a bizarre bit of ego inflation if only we stop and think about it. If we truly love the land then we will love all its species and inhabitants. Loving the land is often a good deal easier than loving our fellow human beings, but it is through love of others that we learn to love the greater universe, both material and non-material. The interdependence of the universe is found at the heart of all Paganism (including Hinduism), within mysticism and in modern physics. The Divine is within us and we are part of the Divine. In coming to an understanding of this, we move into the realms of the Spirit.

Another way of reaching out emotionally is hate. Some traditional Witchcraft books and some feminist Witchcraft books advocate cursing. I have even seen a book written by a feminist academic which criticizes Wicca because it does not 'empower' women to curse men, their patriarchal enemies. This is an extremely silly and irresponsible idea and can only be advocated by those who do not believe magic works. What is important to remember is that magic does work – both on the recipient and on the practitioner. Don't be misled by such nonsense.

Magic is about the use of energy. It involves creating certain energies within ourselves and then sending them out into the world to do their work. It is easy enough to create negative energy. How many people have not cursed a driver who causes them to swerve in the road, or some inadvertent shopper who happens to tread on their foot in a busy store? A little anger can be therapeutic. We swear, curse and stamp our feet and feel a whole lot better. This harms no one. Accumulated anger and the negative energy build up needed to indulge in cursing will make us stressed and ill. People who brood and indulge in hate become hateful. As the psychologist Carl Jung said, we all become like the thing we hate. Nor can we do what we will with impunity. Magic operates according to *Three-fold Law*. The energy that we transmit returns to us but three times as strongly as before. In addition, there are checks and balances within the universe. The universe seeks equilibrium and harmony. If we create negative energy then the universe will choose at some point to short-circuit our efforts, with extremely unpleasant effects.

'If it harms none do what you will' sounds superficially easy, but it can be very difficult. Would you help someone attract an individual he or she had fallen in love with? Traditional Witchcraft abounds in love spells, but is it right to make someone fall in love with somebody when they would not otherwise? Will it lead to unhappiness because deep down the couple are not compatible? Love is more than superficial desire. Unrequited love can rarely be turned into happiness by the power of magic.

Another important principle is that magic must not be a refuge for the lazy. It is pointless to do magical work to help someone get a job if they are not doing what is necessary to find one. Another strange truth is that the longer people are Witches, the less active magic they do. This is because something happens along the way. Wicca teaches us to harmonize ourselves with the greater universe, so that with time the direct action of spell-making becomes less necessary. We learn to know what we really want and to be in the right place at the right time to get it. Experienced Witches find that simply by someone asking them to do something and their thinking about it, then the thing will often come to pass. The important steps have been the individual articulating his or her need and the Witch thinking of a successful outcome occurring.

WHEN IS THE BEST TIME FOR MAGIC?

There is a traditional saying in Witchcraft, 'Better it be when the Moon is full.' The Moon exacts a powerful pull on our world. It is the Earth's only natural satellite and it reflects the light and energy of the Sun. The Moon influences many of our physical rhythms. The Moon takes a *sidereal month* of 27.3 days to complete its revolution relative to the stars. This is the standard period of the human cycle of ovulation.

A *synodic month* is the longer period of 29.5 days from one New Moon to the next that we think of as a lunar month. This month is divided into four phases. At the Dark of the Moon, the Sun and Moon are in the same zodiac sign and are at the same longitude. At First Quarter or Waxing Moon, the Sun and Moon are 90 degrees apart. At Full Moon, they are 180 degrees apart and are in the opposite signs of the zodiac to one another. At Last Quarter or Waning Moon, they are 90 degrees apart once more. The Moon has a powerful effect on our sea tides. This is strongest at the Dark of the Moon, when the Sun and Moon are together in the sky and exert their gravitational pull in the same direction, and at Full Moon when they are tugging in opposite directions. At these times we have our high tides. The low or neap tides occur at the First and Last Quarter.

The Moon's gravitational pull affects not only the sea, but also the liquid within the human body. Haemorrhages and bleeding ulcers are more likely at Full Moon. The Moon also affects the menstrual cycle. The only reason that most modern women's menstrual cycles are not regulated by the Moon is because artificial light at night confuses the process. For some women, irregular periods can be helped by leaving a light on in the bedroom for three nights, starting with the fourteenth day in the menstrual cycle. This will imitate the extra light of the full Moon. The Moon also affects the mating behaviour of simple organisms such as fish and worms.

For religions such as Wicca, which traditionally had most rituals outside at night, then the Full Moon has practical benefits. It is much easier to see your way into and out of a wood when the Moon is Full. However the Moon also affects our psychic abilities. This may be due to its physiological effect, or for more complex reasons; but making magic is much easier when the Moon is Full.

PLANETARY INFLUENCES

Another influence on our magical timing is the planets. Experienced astrologers will calculate to the exact minute the right time to carry out a magical act so as to best harness particular planetary energies. This need not concern us here, but we can work with the planetary energies by knowing their attributes and doing our magic on the day of the week that is most appropriate. Each of the seven days of the week is ruled by a different planet. In traditional astrology, our Earth's Moon was considered a planet and the outer planets were unknown. Uranus, Neptune and Pluto play little part therefore in traditional magic. The seven planets considered important are the Sun, Moon, Mars, Mercury, Jupiter, Venus and Saturn.

The Sun is associated, of course, with Sunday, with solar deities and with the colours of the Sun – gold and golden yellow. Solar energy is life-enhancing. It brings wealth and good health.

Monday is 'Moon-day'. The Moon is associated with tides, changes, the health of the human body and our psychic abilities. All the traditional lunar Goddesses of witchery, such as Hecate, are associated with the Moon. Monday is therefore appropriate for magic associated with healing and psychic development. The Moon's colours are white and violet. Think of a Full Moon at night and you will get an idea of its energy. For healing, it is most appropriate when we have to soothe a fever, restore balance to the different systems of the body, or to heal women's gynaecological problems.

The English word 'Tuesday' comes from the Northern European God 'Tiw' or 'Tyr', God of War. His Roman equivalent is Mars. Mars is often known as the 'red planet' because of the red tinge it can have in the night time sky. Red is a colour associated in the human psyche with anger, fire, energy, physical strength. If we need to energize our lives, we can work with Mars energy, but it is important to remember that Mars is a God

74   of War. We must be careful when we seek to draw this kind of energy into our lives. We do not want to overdo it and find ourselves having arguments with everyone around us.

Wednesday is 'Woden' or 'Odin's Day'. Woden or Odin was a patron of the mind, communication and knowledge. His Roman equivalent is Mercury, God of messages and communication. He has a winged helmet and winged sandals which allow him to fly through the air at great speed – as fast as the power of thought. He is also the God of commerce and trade. The colours associated with Mercury are bright, energizing and designed to stimulate the mind rather than the emotions. They are yellow or orange.

Thursday is 'Thor's Day'; also associated with the Roman God Jupiter. His colour is blue, the colour of the sky. Jupiter was King of the Gods and has not only the positive qualities of kingship – love of country and people – but also of prosperity, good humour and love of life. Another name for Jupiter is 'Jove'. Our English word 'jovial' comes from this and will give you an idea of his energy.

Friday comes from the Goddess Freya whose Roman equivalent is Venus, the beautiful planet who appears at evening and at dawn as a bright shining star near the horizon. Venus was the Roman Goddess of beauty and love. Her colour is green, the colour of growth and fertility. Some American books will tell you to use green for money magic. This derives from the idea that American Dollars are green and that by working with the colour green you will increase them. This may work in the US, but the magical logic is lacking elsewhere.

Saturday is 'Saturn's Day'. Saturn is depicted as an old man who is responsible for the time-keeping of the universe. His qualities are carefulness, caution, conservation. He is the opposite of the generous and sometimes spendthrift energy of Jupiter. His colours are dark and earthy – brown and black. In traditional astrology, Saturn has a bad reputation as a planet of melancholy, but this is undeserved. All the planets have both their positive and negative characteristics.

Below is a chart of correspondences for each of the seven planetary energies.

Days of the Week	Planetary Ruler	Planetary Symbol	Oils	Colour	Magical Correspondences
Sunday	Sun	☉	Frankincense	Yellow, gold	Wealth, health
Monday	Moon	☽	Camphor	White, violet	Psychic matters, healing
Tuesday	Mars	♂	Ginger	Red	Strength
Wednesday	Mercury	☿	Lavender	Yellow, orange	Wisdom, teaching, the mind
Thursday	Jupiter	♃	Cedar	Blue	Good fortune, prosperity, good humour
Friday	Venus	♀	Almond	Green	Love
Saturday	Saturn	♄	Earth perfumes: e.g. storax, dittany of Crete	Brown	Stability, earthing, to save money

Planetary Correspondences

USING MAGICAL ABILITIES

Magic depends on our being in a relaxed state and ready to use our energies. To be relaxed we need peace and solitude. It is impossible to do magic if we are worried about someone rushing into the room in the middle, or the telephone ringing or a neighbour visiting. We have to make sure that we will not be disturbed by choosing a time we can be alone and switching off the phone. If we can never get our home to ourselves, then we have to convince our family or friends that we must be allowed some time undisturbed and that if we put a notice on the door saying, 'Meditation in progress, please do not disturb.' It means exactly that. It is important on the practical level that if we want to do magic we must have time and space, but it is also important on a psychol-ogical level. Taking time out to do something for ourselves sends an important signal to the unconscious – that we are someone who is worth spending our own time on. Many people live lives that are totally at the beck and call of others – bosses, partners, children, friends. To take just 20 minutes a day to say, 'This is my time when I am going to do what I want', is an act of self-assertion and empowerment – and an important beginning of magic.

Once we have our private space, we need to create an atmosphere conducive to using our magical powers. Mundane things such as cleanliness and tidiness can help. One sure way of attracting the attention of Witch Hunters was to be seen washing. In the England of Elizabeth I, laws had to be enacted to ensure that apprentices washed all over at least once a year. Magic, however, has always been associated with scrupulous cleanliness. In part, this is a courtesy to the Gods; in part it helps us. We can concentrate much better when we are not in a messy, untidy atmosphere.

Another important reason for creating the right type of space is that magic is about control. This does not mean that magic is for obsessives who need to be in control of everything around them; nor does it mean that we are megalo-maniacs who have to have everyone and everything in our power. What magic is about is taking charge of our lives. How can we do this, if we are not in charge of our everyday environment? Sorting out the space around us before we begin a piece of magic is important.

TRADITIONAL SPELLCRAFT

There are many traditional ways of doing magic which are frequently used in Wicca – cord magic, chanting, wild ecstatic dance, talismans. There are too many to describe fully here, but there is one simple traditional method which is a good point to start. This is candle magic. Below is a description of how to do candle magic, but before trying out some magic for yourself, you need to think about what you are trying to achieve.

THE MAGICAL DECISION PROCESS

Any act of magic requires us to make a number of decisions. These can be related to the five elements as illustrated overleaf.

Earth ▽
Let's start with Earth. What do we want to happen on the material plane? Making this decision requires us to do some practical thinking and decision making about what is realistic and exactly what it is we want.

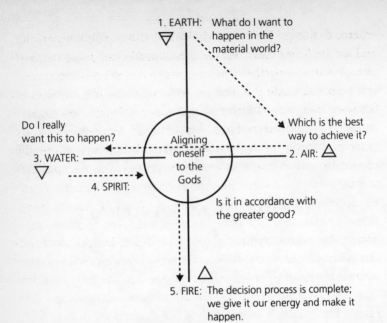

The Magical Decision Process

Air △
What is the best way of achieving it? What do we need to do in terms of constructing a spell? What are the right time, materials, colour correspondences, symbols?

Water ▽
Do we really want it to happen? Do we care enough? Do we have enough emotional involvement? To make magic, we have to be concerned about the result. To do this for other people requires us to be able to reach out to them and empathize with them. We have to be able to love.

Spirit/Ether ✸
We may want something; we may want something for someone else; but is it in accordance with the greater good, the overall

scheme of things? We cannot do just what we want with magic and act with impunity. We have to consider all angles of the situation and all parties involved, not just ourselves or the person who has made the magical request. There is a difference between traditional Witchcraft and modern Wicca here. Ideas of morality and ethics have evolved over the centuries and those of Wicca have evolved with them. A traditional Witch a few centuries ago might have been happy to take payment for putting a curse on someone. His colleague in the next village would then be happy to take a payment from the cursed individual to take the curse off again. While this is a creative solution to the unemployment problem, Wicca today does not do this. Our magic must be done in accordance with a greater scheme of things than one individual viewpoint.

Fire △

If our magical request does hold up to this scrutiny, then it is time to act and to apply our magical energy. We enter the realm of Fire, the realm of will, and we apply our energy to our intent.

SIMPLE EXERCISES TO BEGIN

CANDLE MAGIC

Now you have thought through what you want to do, you need to apply some of the techniques learned in the practice exercises. Before trying out candle magic, for a week or so, practise opening and closing the chakras, and channelling energy into your hands.

Candle magic is a simple and traditional magical technique. Candle magic is a gentle magic. The flame burns and our intent slowly comes into manifestation. It is good for drawing positive energy into our own lives and those of other people. The candle is not essential. We can do the same thing with visualization alone, but the candle helps us focus on our intent.

Candle magic can also be useful if people ask us to do magic for them. A candle can be consecrated and anointed for the individual's intent and he or she can burn it themselves.

1. The first stage of candle magic is to decide on our intent. This is not as easy as it sounds. What exactly do you want? You need to think about this. The next stage is to create a visual image which represents you achieving your intent. This is very important. You need to create a visualization which shows the event as having happened. If you are doing candle magic for someone who is ill, visualize them well, healthy and walking about again. If you are doing candle magic to get a particular job, visualize opening a letter which tells you that you have the job.

2. The second stage is to select an appropriate colour candle. The third stage is to decide an appropriate day on which to begin the magic. Have a look back at the table in Figure 6 (*see page 75*) which will give you some ideas.

3. When you have decided what you want to do and the most appropriate day and candle colour, you need to create a quiet space with an atmosphere conducive to relaxation. Unplug your telephone or put on your answer machine. Choose a time when friends or neighbours are unlikely to drop by.

4. Prepare an altar with symbols of the four elements on it and anything else you feel appropriate. You will need some candles for light as well as a new candle for your candle magic. You will also need some oil to anoint your candle and a spare candlestick for the new candle. You can buy an appropriate aromatherapy or magical oil, using the guide in Figure 6 or you can use a neutral all purpose oil such as pure olive oil from the supermarket.

5. Draw the curtains to block out any light and light the altar candles. You do not have to do your candle magic at night,

but bright light is not conducive to the light trance state you want to achieve in order to focus your magical will.

6. Incense is helpful. You can buy or make an appropriate planetary incense, or you can use a general all purpose incense which appeals to you. As well as burning incense, playing soft music will help you relax. It will also help mask any sudden sounds which might startle you out of your meditative state.

7. Now open your chakras, remembering to keep on drawing energy into the base of spine chakra at various points during your magic.

8. Now you need to think about your magic. Visualize your intent and at the same time channel energy into your hands. Take your candle and hold it for a few moments, focusing on your intent.

9. Now take the anointing oil and put a small amount on your fingers. Oil is a substance which is used in magic to carry energy. Energize your base of spine chakra and draw energy into your hands once more. Now you are going to anoint the candle. Start in the middle and smooth the oil towards each end of the candle. Take more oil if necessary. While you anoint the candle, focus on your intent and create a visual image of your wish coming to pass. Avoid getting the oil on the wick of the candle if you can. It will make it splutter.

10. Now use the candle which is already burning on your altar to light your new candle. Place it in its candlestick. Now ask the Goddess and God to bless your magical intent. You can use your own words for this, saying what is in your heart, or you can say something like this:

Lady and Lord, bless this my intent
and bring it to birth on the Earthly plane.
So mote it be!

11. The candle can now be left to burn for a period. Usually candles are not burned in one session but are burned over a period which you have decided beforehand. This can be a period of a week – if you start on a Sunday you would burn the candle in roughly equal amounts every day finishing on the next Sunday – or over the period of a lunar month. You will have to decide what is the most appropriate period to choose. If you know you are dealing with a complex situation which has been going on for a long time, then you will need to take a longer time.

12. The most difficult part of candle magic is discipline – making yourself burn the candle in this regular pattern. People are always keen to do magic, but few people have the concentration and will power to keep up such a simple thing as lighting a candle every evening over a period of eight days. If we cannot do this, then we do not have sufficient will to bring about the change we seek. The simplest things are always the hardest and bringing change into our lives is hard indeed. How much easier to stay in our rut.

13. When we burn candles in candle magic, we do not have to focus on the candle all the time it is burning. However, we must think about our intent each time we light the candle and when we extinguish it. Once relit, the candle can be left to burn: as long as we take practical precautions to make sure it is safe. Do not leave magical candles near curtains or anything else that might blow into the flame.

14. Each time you put out your candle, think about your intent for a final time. As you extinguish the candle, here are some things you can say:

As I extinguish this flame on the Earthly plane,
may it burn more brightly in the realm of spirit
and bring my intent to birth.

Strong as the wind is my will,
strong as fire is my desire,
strong as the sea, my spell shall be,
strong as the Earth which gives it birth.
so mote it be!

15. At this point you extinguish the flame. In some magical tra-
    ditions, candles are snuffed out rather than blown out. This
    is because the magical theory is that one element (Air, the
    breath) should not be used to extinguish another (the Fiery
    flame). This is not the case in Wicca where the emphasis is
    on the Elements' interaction rather than their separateness.

Note

1. Roberto Assagioli, *Loving Understanding*, quoted in Jean Hardy,
   A Psychology with a Soul: Psychosynthesis in Evolutionary Context,
   Arkana 1989, page 42.

THE GODS

I f the four elements are the basis of the material universe, then the fifth element, Ether or Spirit, represents the Divine. This is behind, within and beyond the material universe – that which binds it together and that which sets it free. Many spiritual paths talk of 'believing in God' and the necessity of faith. In Wicca we prefer to talk about the necessity of scepticism. Experience is emphasized over belief, doctrine and dogma.

Wicca is a Pagan religion and ancient Paganism has been defined by modern historians as a matter of cult acts. Our Pagan ancestors performed rites but professed no creed or doctrine. They came together and worshipped and experienced the Divine, but they kept their beliefs to themselves. In the Classical world, there was no Pagan concept of heresy. To Pagans, the Greek word *hairesis* meant a school of thought, not a false and pernicious doctrine. Pagans were not exhorted to have faith. For those brought up on classical Greek philosophy, faith was the lowest type of thought process – the state of mind of the uneducated. Pagans never called themselves *the faithful*. The term remains one of the few ways archaeologists can distinguish Pagan from Jewish and early Christian tombstone inscriptions.

PRINCIPLES OF WICCA

Belief is a different concept within Paganism from that of the monotheisms of Christianity, Judaism and Islam. The Goddess is the principle around which we base our lives. We do not *believe* in her; she just *is*. Despite what theologians may teach, the metaphysical reality of Goddess or God is ultimately untestable by anything our reason can tell us. We have to follow here the intuition of the heart. We can only trust our own experience (rather than what anyone else tells us) and proceed empirically; testing it out. Does it work for us? Does it help us live our lives in a more fruitful way? Does it improve the way in which we relate to our planet, its inhabitants, our friends and family, and ourselves? Does it help us live in harmony with others?

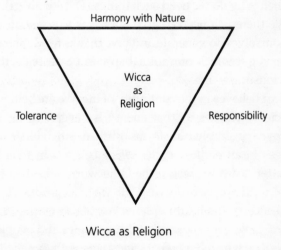

Harmony with Nature

Wicca as Religion

Tolerance

Responsibility

Wicca as Religion

To create world harmony, religious tolerance is extremely important. Wicca does not set itself up to be the be all and end all or the only way. Religious and spiritual traditions are evolving and represent the peak of human understanding of our universe at a particular time and in a particular culture. The sum of human knowledge has not yet been reached.

Tolerance must be aligned with responsibility. Many people today are sceptical about spiritual systems and rightly so. Religions and creeds have promised too much – that they were the only right way; that they would promote love and tolerance when they do exactly the opposite; that they were concerned about humanity when all they were interested in was their own powers and privileges. Wicca puts the responsibility for running our lives back where it belongs – in our own hands. We must take responsibility for our own spiritual development. No one else can do it for us.

Religion, worship, Gods – these are strange words in our post-modernist world ruled by computer technology, a creeping global mono-culture and the all-pervading power of the Internet. Why do we need such things? Deep within the human psyche there is a need to give ourselves to something greater than ourselves; to venerate and give thanks for this strange and precious gift which our animal species possesses – the gift of consciousness – life.

Wicca believes in the continuity of life. We are beings of energy. Science teaches us that energy is never lost. It cannot be destroyed; it simply transforms. Birth, death, rebirth; our being changes in an endless cycle. Wicca believes in reincarnation; that after death we rest in the Otherworld and then incarnate again, until we have learned all that we need to know and experience on the Earthly plane. Wicca also teaches the power of love. Love is an energy that draws things and people together; it is a tie which binds. We reincarnate with those with whom we have made lasting ties. Our Gods teach that we shall meet and know and love them again.

Wicca does not teach reincarnation in exactly the same way as, say, Buddhism. It does not say that we evolve through different species. It tends to focus on reincarnation within the human family. This does not, of course, mean that other transformations and progressions are not possible. However, often our ancestors believed in reincarnation down the ancestral line. This made having children particularly important – they would be the vehicles for our own return. Gerald Gardner believed that Witches reincarnated not down their physical family line, but down the spiritual line of their initiatory tradition. Interestingly, no one to my knowledge has yet claimed to be the reincarnation of Gerald Gardner, but no doubt one day it will occur!

Reincarnation is not always an attractive prospect. Sometimes life can be grim – things go wrong, relationships disintegrate, we find it difficult to get work, our television news is full of war and misery. To affirm the value of life, the joy of existence against all this can seem madness. But life is a joy and a great gift and strangely enough it is often those who lives are most desperate and terrible who show us just how precious a gift it is. The psychiatrist Dr Viktor Frankl, who trained under the American witch Margot Adler's grandfather, Alfred Adler, was imprisoned in various Nazi death camps. In one of his books, he described the death of a young woman in one of the camps.

This young woman knew she would die in the next few days. But when I talked to her she was cheerful in spite of this knowledge...

Pointing through the window of the hut, she said, 'This tree here is the only friend I have in my loneliness.'

Through that window she could see just one branch of a chestnut tree, and on the branch were two blossoms.

'I often talk to this tree,' she said to me.

I was startled and didn't quite know how to take her words. Was she delirious? Did she have occasional hallucinations? Anxiously

I asked her if the tree replied.

'Yes.'

What did it say to her? She answered, 'It said to me, "I am here –
I am here – I am life, eternal life." '[1]

Yes, within the tree is life. This was not a Wiccan who saw this
but an ordinary person living in extraordinary circumstances
who, close to losing her own life, could see that life itself was of
value. It is this value that we have for each individual existence, for the unfolding of the life force in its never ending
mystery, for the beauty of star, mountain, sunset, child, flower,
song, that show to us the extraordinary wonder of what the
Gods have given us. For this we give them thanks.

THE GODS

But first – who and what do we worship? Wicca is the *Old
Religion*. We worship the earliest forms of deity that the human
mind and heart conceived – the Great Mother Goddess and her
consort the Horned God. Wicca is similar to other religions in
that we have rites and ceremonies to worship our deities, but
deities not *a* God.

In the Age of Pisces, the last 2,000 years, the trend was
towards *monotheism* – a simplification of the Divine Reality
into a single male God. The reasons for this are complex –
political, historical and those of esoteric astrology. However,
this distorted reality. It created a climate of intolerance in
which there is only one acceptable form of the Divine. This is
the form sanctioned by the dominant religious and political
authorities in each country. In such systems, other people's
deities are seen as evil.

Wicca recognizes that other people's Gods are part of the Divine mystery. The Divine Reality is many-faceted. Wicca's own Gods appear in different guises in the faiths of all peoples. In Native American pueblo tradition the Great Mother Goddess appears as Spider Woman who weaves the world. In Christianity she is the Virgin Mary; in Hinduism she is Kali and Laksmi; in Tibetan Buddhism she is Green Tara.

Wicca worships Goddess and God, but humanoid images are ways for us to approach and understand a greater mystery – that the different images we have worshipped over the aeons are creations of the human mind. They are ways for us to approach the ineffable mystery – the one great spirit that gives life to the universe. In Wicca, this is often called the life force, the Divine, the essence, the power that moves the Universe. It is outside us, beyond us; yet within our innermost selves. We see its work in the changing face of Nature, the seasonal cycle that echoes the pattern of the universe – creation, maturation, decay, death and rebirth.

In many cultures all over the world, Nature is seen as Goddess. In European languages, the words for Nature are feminine – *phusis* in Greek, *natura* in Latin, *la nature* in French, *die Natur* in German. The Greek philosopher Plato saw the Goddess as the soul of the world. It is easy to see how the connection is made between Nature, the Great Mother, the Womb of the Earth, fertility.

Outside Europe, the idea of Earth as mother was common. This was one reason many traditional peoples had strong reservations about the 'benefits' of Western civilization and its mechanistic attitudes to the Earth. Anthropologist Mircea Eliade, in his book *The Sacred and Profane*, describes the reaction of a chief of the Native American Wanapum tribe towards Western attitudes to agriculture and mining.

Should a knife tear my mother's bosom?
       Then when I die she will not take me to her bosom and rest.
       You ask me to dig for stone!
       Shall I dig under her skin for bones?
       Then when I die I cannot enter her body again.
       You ask me to cut grass and make hay and sell it,
       and be rich like white men!
       But how dare I cut off my mother's hair.[2]

The association of Nature with the feminine is not all good. The equation of *woman = Nature = soil to be ploughed* reflects a mindset in Western society that encourages the exploitation by male-dominated society of both women and Nature. Wicca does not equate Nature solely with the feminine in this way. Wicca tends to see different aspects of Nature as more masculine or more feminine but not consistently so. 'Male' and 'female' are human-made constructs. Our Gods do not have gender. We may choose to portray and understand them as Goddess and God, female and male. However, these are but ways for the human mind to grapple with and come to an intuitive understanding of the Divine force which is beyond gender.

Symbols that equate the Moon with Goddess, Earth and passivity, tend to reflect the society around them. They are not absolutes, but symbols and no more than that. In Wicca, the Moon may be seen as the young God, the offspring of the Great Sun Goddess; or the Moon may be seen as the Triple Goddess. Sometimes the Goddess is seen as the Moon and the God as the vegetation, the seeds which grow according to the Moon's power. Different sets of symbolism work at different times.

Our earliest ancestors made crude Goddess figures like this:

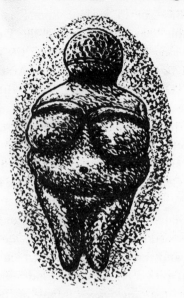

The Willendorf Venus

These Goddesses were big women. They had rounded bellies. Their sexual and fertility organs – breasts and vulva – were emphasized; for fertility was essential to the life of the people. There must be children to carry the life of the tribe forward and to grow up and care for those older than themselves. Today we live in a world of ruthless individualism, but this was not the world of our ancestors. Every member of the tribe was dependent on everyone else and responsible for everyone else. And all were dependent on the Gods who brought new life and who received us into death.

In the West, Goddess worship was suppressed by centuries of monotheism. However, if we look further back we find the Great Mother, worshipped in Ephesus as many-breasted Artemis; in Egypt as Isis whose veil might be lifted by none; as Cybele, Great Mother Goddess of Asia Minor whose worship was brought to ancient Rome; as Inanna of the Sumerians – she who descends into the Underworld and overcomes the forces of death. In Wicca, the Goddess is still worshipped in her ancient names – as Aradia, Cerridwen, Isis, Astarte, Dione, Melusine, Aphrodite, Dana and Arianrhod. She can be called by all these different names because these are but some of the many names under which the Mighty Mother of us All has been known throughout the millennia. She appears in Egypt in her form as the Great Cat Goddess Bast, Goddess of love, whose black statues can still be bought today. She is Venus in her Roman aspect of love Goddess and Diana in her form as the Virgin Huntress of the Moon who is owned by no man. She is Hecate the Goddess of the crossroads and the August storms which may blight the harvest. She is Aphrodite, the Greek Goddess of love, born it is said from the foaming waves. Many of the names of the Goddess have an 'Ah' sound, the soothing sound of the mother: Arianrhod, Annis, Anu, Aradia.

Traditionally, the Wiccan Goddess is worshipped in Triple form – as the Virgin who has not yet known motherhood or who has not chosen this path, as the Mother, and as the Wise Woman, who is post-motherhood, she who acts as midwife to the Mother and as layer out at Death. These three aspects of the Goddess are represented by the waxing, Full and waning Moons. Our deity images reflect the reality of our lives and for women today, the Triple Goddess may no longer be appropriate. Another way of thinking about the Goddess in Wicca is not as a trinity but as that most Wiccan of symbols – the pentagram.

THE GODDESS AS PENTAGRAM

A woman's life can be seen as a journey around the pentagram.

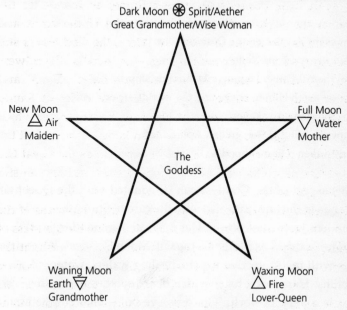

The Goddess as Pentagram

In our youth, we learn the lessons of Air, the lessons of the intellect, which we need to carry us into the outer world. With Air we have the true Virgin Goddesses of learning and wisdom who forsake the life of the passions for the life of the mind. The great Abbesses of Medieval Europe such as Hildegard von Bingen were women in this mould. The magical command of this phase of our lives is: To Know. We must learn.

With puberty we enter the world of sexuality and passion, the realm of Fire. This is the Goddess as Lover-Queen. She is not the Virgin or the Mother, but the woman in charge of her own destiny and her sexuality. In the East, in the Tantric

scriptures, we find reference to this aspect of the Goddess and also in the work of Western female magicians. It is She of whom the great magician Dion Fortune wrote:

Golden Aphrodite cometh not as the Virgin, the victim,
but as the Awakener, the Desirous One.
As outer space She calls,
and the All-Father commences the courtship.
She awaketh Him to desire and the worlds are created.
Lo, She is the Awakener.
How powerful is She, golden Aphrodite,
the awakener of manhood!

This aspect of the Goddess can be equated with the Queen of Wands in the tarot and also with the card of Strength – an independent woman of power. Her magical command is: To Will.

The Goddess as Mother is the Full Moon Goddess. We equate her with the protective waters, healing waters, waters of tranquillity. Hers is the hand which heals, soothes and calms. The sea is a very powerful Goddess symbol – changing, eternal, powerful, speaking of the cycles of creativity. Her command is: To Dare. For motherhood we must be brave; not only to endure the physical rigours of pregnancy and childbirth, but to bring a new life into the world and to nurture it in these difficult times. To parent is an act of courage. We must overcome our own fears and defend our young. This is the way of the Goddess Mother.

The fourth aspect of the Goddess is the Waning Moon Goddess whose element is Earth. Here we have the magical commandment: To Keep Silent. The Grandmother Goddess is the figure who has seen all of life's difficulties and has triumphed over them. This gives her inner strength and the wisdom to help others who are going through the same problems. She is the Wise Woman who

The Phases of the Goddess

knows the hidden secrets of the Earth. She sits in her cottage
deep in the woods and we must go to her if we wish to learn
her wisdom. Her command is: To Keep Silent. When we are
silent we hear.

The fifth aspect of the Goddess is not the grey-haired grandmother but the Dark Goddess, the shrouded Goddess of death
whose face we do not see until we lift the veil between this
world and the next. This is Great Grandmother Goddess. Hers
is the point of death, rebirth and initiation. We enter the rapture
of the spirit rather than that of the flesh and participate in the
mysteries of the Gods. This is a hard phase, the hardest; for to
reach it we will have suffered much in life. Awe, despair, fear,
emptiness – these too are part of the road to knowledge. The
image of the labyrinth is appropriate here; so too is the cauldron which symbolizes some of the mysteries of initiation. This
is the realm of ether or spirit, the realm of spirituality, the realm
of the priestess.

Goddess Phase	Moon Phase	Goddess	Element	Season	Quality	Magical Command	Magical Weapon
Maiden	New	Persephone	Air	Imbolc	Joy, creation, the song, the head	To know (to expand the mind)	Knife
Lover	Waxing	Aphrodite, Bride, Freya, Kali, Nephthys	Fire Beltane	Spring, Equinox	Passion, union, vagina	To will (to assert and express ourselves)	Wand
Mother	Full	Hera, Isis	Water	Mid-summer, Yule	Love, sustenance, womb	To dare (to brave physical rigours and to overcome fear)	Cup
Grand-mother	Waning	Demeter, Frigga (she knows every-one's fate)	Earth	Lammas, Autumn Equinox	Sorrow, separation, letting go	To keep silent (in order to digest and learn)	Shield
Wise One/ Dark Great Grand-mother		Hecate, Cerridwen	Aether/ spirit	Samhain	Wisdom, death, rest, transforma-tion, rebirth, initiation	To teach, to reveal	Cauldron, Crystal ball

The Five-fold Goddess

Some will explore this realm in later life when obligations of family and career have been fulfilled. Others will establish first their spirituality before seeking relationships or a career, but whenever in our lives we choose to address them, the demands of the spirit are strong and if we ignore them a dimension of our lives will be missing. Her commands are: To Teach; To Reveal.

GOD

The God in Wicca is co-equal with the Goddess and an essential part of the Wiccan world view. Deep within the deepest caves, through dark passages with only the light of flickering and unreliable torches to guide us, we find the image of the God of hunt and forest, Lord of the Beasts, drawn by our earliest Stone Age ancestors. Here are beautiful animated paintings of animals, those animals most needed for the hunt and therefore

The Horned God

98   most sacred – bison, deer, elk, mammoth. And also that most powerful and mysterious figure – the Horned God – with the horns of an animal, cloven feet and the body of a man. I say the horns of an animal, but this is not the whole truth. To our ancestors horns were a symbol of power and strength and therefore of divinity.

The Horned God appears in many different cultures throughout the world. In India, he is Parvati, Lord of the Animals; he is Pan of the Greeks and Cernunnos of the Celts, who in England is known as Herne.

O Herne of the wild hills,
of starlight sky
and pale watching moon.
In northern realms,
where ravens croaking,
Bring forth messages
of life and death:
we call Thee.
Thou who keeps the land and watches;
Guardian of the Forest;
Walker of the Secret Ways,
by glow worm fire and comet's blaze,
by hoot of owl and howling wind,
by fresh green shoot and towering oak
we call Thee: come!

The different aspects of God in Wicca can be most easily understood in terms of the seasonal cycle and of the elements. The God is born as the Sun Child in the depths of winter, the darkest and coldest time. The child is a symbol of hope, continuity, rebirth, the struggle of life against death. He symbolizes all that is new and renewing. He emerges into the World.

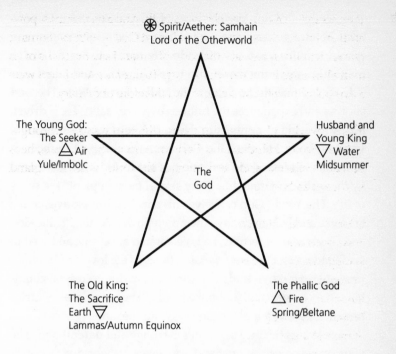

The God

As the young God he comes forth, seeking, curious, not yet part of the emotional realm. He is the young Airy playful God who wants no ties, only freedom. This is the God aspect that we need to experience the joys of life – laughter, dance, Pan as Player of the Pipes is he. His is curiosity and inventiveness. He is the God of Imbolc, which takes place in the sign of Aquarius. In Celtic Wicca, Imbolc is often the festival when the young God receives his arms. A young priestess will choose a man to represent the God at the next festival of Spring Equinox.

'Come forth that we may arm you,' invites the priestess to the chosen one. He is given the sword of Nuada, the spear of Lugh, and he drinks of the Cup of the Wine of Life, the Cup of

sacrifice. In this is a premonition of what is to come. This the stage of adolescence, when in traditional societies a young man would acquire his tools of trade. He wants to learn how to make his way in the world and to use his skills and talents.

In Springtime, the Sun enters the zodiac sign of Aries. The God evolves and experiences the fullness of his sexuality. He is driven not by love, but by animal lust. He knows the joys of a strong and youthful body. He seeks the Goddess – or maybe a number of different Goddesses! He seeks no ties but finds himself ensnared by the realities of daily life. Fiery sexual passion plants the seeds of life. The Young God conceives his son. The imperatives of the life force and of Nature have their own power. As the Phallic God and Green Man of fertility, he is celebrated at Beltane and wed to the Goddess and the land. Passion turns to the love and binding-ness of Water. Love leads to caring and caring to responsibility. He can no longer think of himself alone. The young male warrior becomes the servant of the Goddess and the land.

Love brings ties and ties bring marriage and parenthood. The warrior becomes the husband and takes on worldly responsi-bilities. In Celtic myth the role of the King is associated always with that most watery of symbols the Cup or the Grail. We drink of this draught and see all life's richness – joy and sor-row. We know strength and pain, the pain of connectedness, empathy, of feeling the sufferings of others close to us. Paradoxically, in the northern hemisphere, the sun is at its height at Midsummer when it enters the sign of Cancer the Crab – a water sign. Fire and Water meet and therein lies the mystery. All kingly Gods are associated with this aspect.

The God is the energy and power within the land. As sum-mer passes so the land becomes dry and arid. The greenness of spring and early summer turns to brown. The heat of the sun brings death and ageing. The king is past his prime and his power weakens. The full flesh of youth becomes a dried and

arid husk. Water gives way to Earth. Here we have the myth of sacrifice – that to move forward we must let go of the past. This is the Celtic myth of the Fisher King who can be healed only by the Grail. This is the corn God who must be slain so that the people may be fed. This is the midpoint of life and the next phase. The body weakens and we must learn to adapt to this. If we do, then the spirit becomes strong.

Nights lengthen, the land grows colder, Autumn comes. The spirit of the slain God walks the land awaiting the Goddess. When she is ready to descend with him to the Underworld, then they depart. Now we have the God of the darkest time, when the Sun declines and each night grows longer. The God re-enters the realm of spirit. Darkness is not a fearful thing in Wiccan mythology. Darkness is the shade from the brightness of the sun, it is the time of sleep, rest, regeneration. The seed must be buried beneath the dark Earth in order to germinate. Darkness is our friend. The days before the Winter Solstice are when the world holds its breath. We await the rebirth of the sun child, so that the God may reappear on Earth again with the next spring. Another way of seeing his journey is illustrated overleaf:

The God emerges out of the centre, the place of darkness, the hidden, the underworld wherein the Goddess give birth. Spirit is incarnate in the flesh of Earth. The young God is born into the world. He journeys through the elements. In his youthful Airy aspect, he obeys the magical command of: To Know. As the young God in his prime, he learns: To Will. As father and husband with responsibility for others, he must overcome the fear of connectedness and must obey the command: To Dare. With the dying of Summer, comes the time of sacrifice. He must let go of worldly achievement if he is to progress and discover more. He enters the Otherworld, the Underworld, via the tomb of Earth, borne like a fallen hero upon his shield. In the place of

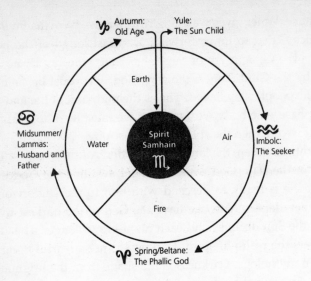

The God's Sabbat Journey

enforced exile away from worldly things, he must rest and learn the command: To Keep Silent. He returns to the centre, the place of Spirit, to return again in the coming year. There in the hidden places, the caves and temples of initiation, he teaches us the Mysteries of the Cauldron, the symbol of the Samhain feast. From him, with his lady the Dark Goddess of Mystery, we learn the meaning of the magical commandments: To teach, to reveal. From darkness, he emerges into light once more, seeking new light, the light that is sought and found. The Dark Lord becomes the Sun Child, the Child of Promise. This is his Spiral Dance.

Season	God Phase	Element	Quality	Magical Command	Moon Phase	Magical Weapon
Imbolc	Child, young God	Air	Joy, creation, the song, the head	To know (to expand the mind)	New	Sword of Nuada
Spring, Equinox, Beltane	Lover, Green Man, Phallic Lord	Fire	Passion, union, phallus	To will (to assert and express ourselves)	Waxing	Staff, rod Spear of Lugh
Mid-summer, Yule	Husband, Father, King	Water	Love, sustenance	To dare (to brave physical rigours and to overcome fear)	Full	Cup
Lammas, Autumn Equinox	Old God, Sacrifice	Earth	Sorrow, separation, letting go	To keep silent (in order to digest and learn)	Waning	Shield
Samhain	Dark Lord, Initiator, Lord of Death	Aether/ spirit	Wisdom, death, rest transformation, rebirth, initiation	To teach, to reveal	Dark	Cauldron, crystal ball

The Five-fold God

These then are images of Goddess and God to help you understand the nature of Wiccan worship. We venerate with each season's change the aspect of the Goddess and God appropriate to that time. Thus do we honour the cycles and seasons of existence. Both life and death are honoured, and always behind both is the message of hope – the message of rebirth. We live, we die, we live again. To develop further in Wicca, we must begin to build a relationship with the Gods. You may feel that you have already encountered the Goddess and God through dream, meditation, prayer, ritual or an experience in Nature. Below are two exercises to help you strengthen your links with the Divine.

SIMPLE EXERCISES TO BEGIN

ATTUNING OURSELVES TO THE DIVINE

These are two inner journeys to contact the Goddess and God. You will need to visualize the scene described and then allow your mind to go on an inner journey. You can do the exercises outdoors in some quiet and peaceful spot. Indoors, you will need quiet and subdued lighting. You may find it helpful to play appropriate music, burn incense and light a candle. Begin each exercise by opening your chakras. At the end of each exercise, record your experiences; otherwise like dreams you will forget them. Then close your chakras and earth yourself by eating and drinking something. Do not do both exercises on the same day as you will get less out of them. The exercises will work best if you memorize them for a day to two beforehand, so you do not have to look at the instructions and so break your concentration.

GODDESS PATHWORKING

1. Visualize that you are standing in front of a black curtain on which is a silver moon. Hold this image in your mind for a little while.

2. Now imagine that the black curtain is becoming a transparent black veil through which you can see a landscape. On the other side of the veil you can see a path through the landscape.

3. Ask the permission of the Goddess to enter her kingdom and ask her to show you some of her secrets and symbols. Now part the veil, step through it and begin to follow the path. You are journeying into the Goddess' kingdom to meet with her in some sacred place of her choosing. When you feel you have reached the right place, stop and rest, and await her coming. If she appears she may have some message for you.

4. When you are ready to leave, bid the Goddess farewell if she has not already departed. Return to the veil and step back through it.

GOD EXERCISE

1. You find yourself in a meadow at the base of a green hill. It is evening. The sun is setting and the last rays of light are disappearing behind the hill. As the sky grows darker, the stars begin to appear. A Full Moon begins to rise above the horizon. Its rays cast a soft silver light over the meadow bathing you in a feeling of gentleness and peace.

2. A soft breeze blows down the hillside. On it you can hear the faint sound of drumming. You want to know the source of the sound. You cross the meadow and begin to climb the hill.

3. When you reach the top, you see a circle of standing stones ahead of you. There are people there, some standing and some seated in the circle. As you draw near, they become aware of you, but you are welcome. A space is made for you inside the circle.

4. Then, from the other side of the circle, a figure appears and steps into the centre of the circle. He is very tall and on his head you see the antlers of a stag. There is a fire burning near the centre of the circle and its flames light up his face.

5. The circle falls silent. The people are waiting for him to speak. And then you hear his voice speaking softly. It is as though he is whispering in your ear and speaking to you alone. He is calling you to come to him.

6. You cross the circle and find yourself standing beside the tall horned figure. He emanates great power, but also a great sense of gentleness. Then the God reaches out his hand and you sit down beside him by the fire.

7. You sit together, gazing into the flames. Pictures begin to form in your mind of his world – the world of the powers behind the veil of Nature, the energy of stones, of animals, of trees. Allow him to tell you all that he feels you need to know.

8. The sky grows lighter. Dawn is approaching. Your time together is coming to an end. You bid him farewell and then leave the stone circle. You find yourself walking down the hillside to the meadow below. The sun is rising. You reach the meadow as the first rays of morning sun are beginning to warm the grass and dry the dew.

Notes

1. Viktor E Frankl, *Man's Search for Meaning: An introduction to logotherapy*, Touchstone ed, 1984, pages 77–8.

2. Mircea Eliade, *The Sacred and Profane: The Nature of Religion*, Harcourt, Brace and World, NY 1959, page 138.

7

CREATING RITUAL

Now that you know more about the Gods and about the seasonal cycle of Wicca, you can begin to think about creating rites of worship. Perhaps you would like to do ritual but do not have space or privacy. It is important to remember that you do not have to perform ritual outwardly. You can perform ritual in the tiniest of rooms if necessary. You can cast a circle purely by visualization. This is a good exercise in concentration. Every now and then, more experienced Witches will do a ritual this way just to keep their minds well-trained.

Dressing in a robe, learning words and performing ritual actions can seem strange; especially if we stop and think about it. Try not to think too much – especially in the middle of a rite. We have to enter our ritual space with trust and open-mindedness and just see what happens. The strange and interesting part is that things do happen which have no logical explanation. After a while we just get used to it and find that travelling the universe in a Buddhist type of 'not knowing' is really OK.

Wiccan ritual varies between different traditions, but if you read a number of books about Witchcraft, you will find that rituals do have a certain pattern. The words for casting a circle may vary, but the idea that rites take place within a consecrated space called the circle will be common to all Wiccan traditions. Deity names vary but the idea of Goddess and God runs through the traditions. Some covens and traditions use a particular name for the Goddess and the God all the time. Others change the name according to the season or phase of the Moon to emphasize that they are calling upon different aspects of the Divine force. The God is usually addressed as Herne, Cernunnos or Pan; the Goddess as Bride, Cerridwen, Aradia or Diana. It may be that certain names appeal to you more and you will wish to use these. If not, then try out different male/female pairs until you find what is the right combination for you.

WHAT DO I WEAR?

Perhaps this is a question we might ask before our first teenage party, meeting the potential in-laws or an important job interview; but Wiccan ritual is a special occasion, so – what do people wear?

To create ritual, we need to separate ourselves off from the physical world. We will enter a place *between the worlds* – not quite in the everyday world and not quite outside it. There are

certain conventions that can help us. One is that we wear no
watch and all clocks are banished. Another is that we may
dress slightly differently. We can wear a special robe; we can be
skyclad or naked; or we may simply remove our shoes to show
that we are on sacred ground. When we begin our ritual practice it is enough to remove our shoes and to wash ourselves as
signs that we are making a transition to the 'other realm'.

If you decide that you enjoy ritual, you may wish to buy or
make a robe. As with tools, it is better to make our own; even if
we have to sew them by hand with needle and thread. Green is
a good all-purpose colour. A light-coloured robe is not a good
idea if you want to work ritual outdoors – it will get very dirty.
Nor is it a good idea if you work ritual outdoors at night and
have to be discreet in your outdoor workings. White can be seen
from a long way off. A black outdoor robe and a white indoor
one to which different colour cords can be added for different
types of ritual is a way of being equipped for all occasions. Silk
or cotton is fine for indoor working. Outside, wool or velvet are
good warm materials. If you remember the principle that organic material is a better carrier of etheric energy, you will realize
that natural materials are preferred to artificial ones. They are
also much less likely to melt in front of a ritual fire.

Not everyone feels comfortable with the idea of robes; especially men, who are not used to wearing long flowing gar-
ments. An alternative is to keep some simple clothing that you
use for ritual purposes. Tai chi clothes or similar are possible
and have the advantage that if anyone turns up unexpectedly
it looks as though you are doing some complex form of Eastern
meditation rather than anything more exotic! Much depends,
of course, on whether you do rituals outdoors or in. For outside, you could have a set of clean ordinary clothes in natural
materials for ritual that would not make you look that different
from the average camper when sitting around your ritual fire.

The use of robes in Wicca differs in an important respect from some parts of the Western Magical Tradition. Wiccan robes tend to be simple; whereas those in ritual magic can be quite elaborate. For many magicians, putting on a robe and adopting a magical name is a way of putting on a magical personality or persona – that of a much more powerful person who is very different from our ordinary everyday selves. In Wicca, the symbolism is the opposite. We remove the persona to stand naked before the Gods; or if robed, we drop the everyday personality which we have built up to deal with the world. The aim is to strip away barriers between ourselves and the Gods, rather than to create an exotic magical personality.

CORDS

When working robed or skyclad, Witches usually wear a cord around the waist. This symbolizes that they are bound to the Gods and is a reminder of their dedication to the Craft. The length is nine feet or three metres (the latter is for Euro-witches and larger and/or taller Wiccans will find the extra length better). In many traditions, certain colour cords indicate a certain level of initiation. If you decide to wear a cord for ritual, you do not want to imply that you are claiming status you do not have. Neutral colours that are not used in this way are brown (a good Earthy colour) and white (to symbolize purity of intent). Using either or both of these is recommended at this stage. The cord used is usually furnishing cord. It is the type of thing you may have seen sewn around the edge of velvet cushions. This is usually three-stranded. Alternatively, you could buy three single strands and weave you own cord, using white, brown and one of the other elemental colours which appeal to you – bluey-green for Water, blue for Air or Red for fire. Usually these days cord is made of synthetic fibres. If you want to keep to the rule

of 'everything organic', white cotton cord is usually available
and can be dyed using cold water dyes.

JEWELLERY

Many Witches wear the five-pointed star or the Egyptian ankh
or looped cross as a reminder of their links to the Craft.
Another practice of female Witches is to wear an amber necklace or a necklace of amber and jet. Amber necklaces have been
found in the graves of Bronze Age priestesses. The necklace in
Wicca is known as the 'Necklace of Rebirth'. Its circular shape
is reminiscent of all circles and cycles, including those of conception, birth, death and rebirth.

WHAT DO I NEED?

One popular image of Witches is of mysterious figures dancing
around inside a circle of ancient standing stones at night. This
image has some truth. Wiccan rituals often do take place at
night. They are not always in the romantic outdoor setting of a
stone circle, but they do take place within a circle. The circle is
holy ground or *sacred space* for the duration of the rite. There
will be an altar in either the north of the circle (the north in
European tradition is the home of the Gods) or in the centre
with its back to the north. If the rite is outside, a fire may occu-
py the central position; or if indoors a cauldron.

Creating a circle for a rite is known as 'Casting the circle'.
This involves sanctifying the ritual space with the four elements – Air, Fire, Water and Earth – and sealing it by drawing
a circle around it, either in the air or on the ground using a consecrated magical tool – a wand or an athame.

You will need a candle for Fire, something with the qualities of
lightness or sound for Air, a bowl of water for Water, and earth

or a stone for Earth. You will also need salt and a container for salt; incense and a censer in which to burn it, or an incense stick; and a cup or goblet and a plate for ceremonial drinking and eating at the end of your rite. Finally, you will need a magical tool through which to project your energy. This can be a ritual knife which in Wicca is called an *athame*, or it can be a wand.

WATER AND SALT

Water is consecrated at an early stage in Wiccan ritual. Now piped water has so many chemicals, Witches often keep spring water for rites. You can buy bottled water or you can collect it from special places or sacred sites. Salt is added to the water to consecrate and purify it. Why salt? Salt symbolizes the element of Earth. Salt is a purifying substance which plays an important role in the body's balancing mechanisms. It has long been used for its sterilizing and preservative properties. Pure salt is recommended rather than table salt to which iodine has been added. Rock salt is the most 'earthy' of salts, but sea salt is also appropriate.

At the end of the rite, any unused water is poured into the ground at a spot where the salt will not damage growing plants. Do not pour it down the kitchen sink! Once you have made something sacred, you must treat it with respect. This is important on both a magical and a psychological level. It is important in magic that we learn to respect our own actions and to honour them. By making something sacred we are creating certain boundaries around it and setting it aside. It becomes important for you. If you live on the twenty-fourth floor and are surrounded by concrete, then keep a pot of earth and pour your unused water into this. Every now and then take the earth into the countryside or to a park, tip it out and get new earth.

Having cleansed our ritual space, we perfume it with incense. You can use joss sticks or incense sticks for your incense, but loose incense which is burned on charcoal blocks smells much better. You can buy incense and charcoal in esoteric stores or from mail order suppliers whose addresses you find in esoteric magazines. Alternatively, there is always the ancient occult standby of Catholic church suppliers. What is even better is to make your own. There are some good books on incense making which you can find in esoteric book stores.

If you decide to use loose incense, the charcoal is ignited by holding it in a candle or other flame. Small pliers or sugar tongs are useful here. They will stop your fingers getting burned. Resting the block on a teaspoon with part of it protruding into a candle flame also works. Charcoal blocks become hot and you will need to put a bed of earth or sand in your censer to stop the block burning your hands or altar. Once the block has burned through, loose incense is sprinkled on it and will burn.

Why do we use incense? Our sense of smell is evocative and powerful. Different incenses create different moods and states of consciousness. These can be harnessed for different types of magical work – hence the different planetary incenses that you will find in occult suppliers' catalogues. Different incenses are like different tunes that stimulate different moods and energies within us.

In Wiccan ritual, censing takes place early in the rite and is part of the cleansing process that clears the way for raising magical energies. We use incense both for our own benefit and as a 'sweet-smelling offering to the Gods'. Incense has been used in religious and magical ritual since time immemorial. Censing has always been seen as a sanctification and an important part of setting aside a holy place.

CANDLES

In indoor ritual we use candles to light our sacred space. Most candles today are made of paraffin wax. These are fine but do not have the beautiful and heady aroma of beeswax candles. You may want to try beeswax to see if you prefer it.

One or two candles are usually placed on the altar. Four candles are placed at the edge of the sacred space – one in each of the four quarters or cardinal directions – East, South, West and North.

Most Wiccan traditions use different colours at each quarter. One good system follows the colour of the elements in Nature – thus blue, the colour of sky, is used in the East (Air); red, the colour of Fire, is used in the South (Fire); bluey-green, the colour of the sea is used in the West (Water); and for North (Earth), brown is used, the colour of the soil. For altar candles, use whatever colours seem appropriate for the season or the magical intention.

Why are these particular elements attributed to these cardinal directions? No one is absolutely sure, but this is the system used in European Witchcraft and for the geography of Western Europe, it makes lots of sense. Our biggest expanse of water – the Atlantic Ocean – is to the West. The warmest point, where the Sun is at its height is the South and becomes Fire. Winds often come from the East which is thus Air. Mountainous Scandinavia and Scotland lie to the North. If you live in other parts of the world, your geography will be different and you will have to decide whether the elemental attributions make sense. In the southern hemisphere, most Witches reverse Fire and Earth and put Fire in the North, the position of the noonday sun, and Earth in the South. In Native American tradition, the elemental attributions are different again. However, for your early ritual work, it may be best to stick to the tried and trusted method of the Western magical tradition.

For lighting outdoor ritual, you will need containers that shelter the flame from the wind. One solution is to use lanterns for your altar and quarter lights. Garden torches and garden candles can be used. One advantage of some garden candles is that they include mosquito repellent. While its aroma may not be magically inspiring, neither are mosquito bites. At some times of the year, mosquito repellent is an essential part of the Witches' wardrobe.

ATHAME

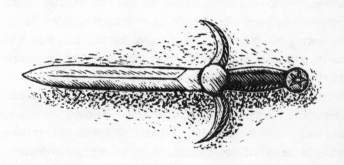

The black-handled ritual dagger, *the athame*, is known as *the true Witch's Weapon*. The origin of the word is obscure but it may come from the Old French *attame* which means to cut or to pierce. The athame is thus the witch's 'cutter and piercer' and attributed to the element of Air. Ideally, we should make our own athames, but few of us are skilful enough to forge a blade. However, even if we buy a ritual knife from an occult supplier, we can still put something of ourselves into it, by carving or painting the handle.

Knives can be dangerous and in some countries there are laws about the type of blade it is legal to own or to carry on

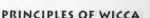

your person. It is a weapon as well as a tool and is a symbol of the Witch's personal magical power. The word 'weapon' is an important reminder that power can be misused. In magic and Wicca we must think before we act.

One way of harmonizing our intentions with the greater good is to consecrate our magical tools to the Gods. This will help ensure that we do not misuse them, but we must not rely on this alone. We need to use our innate gifts of discernment to use magical power wisely and well. One Witchcraft tradition is that no one except our magical partner, if we have one, may use our athame. Our magical tools become imbued with our etheric energy. Etheric energy is stored by organic material, such as wood, beeswax, wool, silk and cotton. The wooden handle of our athame will become imbued with our own magical 'key note'. By not allowing others to touch it, we ensure that it is truly ours. This leads to another point about athames: we should not adopt a ritual knife that has been used for negative purposes. Old military knives are not a good idea. Cooking knives are fine. Some people prefer not to use steel athames at all. There are old superstitions about iron-based metals being aversive to the fairy and other worlds. In some Witchcraft traditions bronze athames are used.

WAND

We do not need to use an athame. Another ancient magical tool which we can use to channel energy is a wand. Wands are attributed to the element of Fire; something which will be familiar to many people from the tarot. If the association is a new one, it may seem strange at first. If you think about it, you will see that the wand can become a burning torch, the light of which travels long distances. In the tarot, wands indicate energy and creative will.

Using wands to cast a circle and invoke the quarters gives a very different energy from using metal blades. It is well worth doing on occasion even if we do not want to do it all the time. My Gardnerian High Priestess preferred wooden athames or wands and sometimes, if we are working ritual outside, a steel blade seems artificial. Natural places may require us to adapt to their gentler energies. An advantage of a wand when we start exploring Wicca is that it is much easier to obtain than an athame. We have simply to go for a walk in the woods to find one.

It is good to do some work on your wand and put something of yourself into it. We may choose to leave the bark on or to scrape it off with a sharp knife. Some Witches carve or paint their wands with runes. A charged crystal can be inserted into the end to direct power or the tip may be whittled to a point. Ritual magic books will tell you that the length of wands should be from your elbow to your finger tip, but this is not the case in Wicca where wands are often longer. The wand is seen as interchangeable with a staff. Some traditions use a particular form of staff with a forked end which is called a stang. This is not used for directing energy – it would go off in two directions at once which would complicate your magic somewhat. Instead, the stang stands in the North of the circle to represent the power of the Horned God.

There is an exercise at the end of the chapter to help you find a wand.

CUP AND PLATE

Wiccan rites usually end with a small celebration – the blessing of cakes or bread and wine. If you want to bless Cakes and Wine in your rites, you will need a chalice or goblet and an ornamental plate or a small basket. These can be found in gift shops or department stores as well as esoteric suppliers. Bread or cakes that you have made yourself are ideal; so too is home-made wine. Mead or ale can also be used. If you prefer not to drink alcohol, use grape or apple juice. Traditionally, the cakes are Moon-shaped crescent biscuits, or at Lammas a newly-baked loaf.

SIMPLE EXERCISES TO BEGIN

FINDING AND CONSECRATING A WAND

You do not need a magical knife, an athame, to begin magical practice, but you will need a traditional Witch's tool through which to channel your energy. You have already learned to channel energy into your hands. This is an essential prerequisite for magical practice. The next step is to learn how to channel your energy into a wand.

What kind of wood is appropriate? This will depend on where you live and what seems to draw you. You can look up the symbolism of different trees in a book such as Robert Graves *The White Goddess*[1] or Jacqueline Memory Paterson's lovely book *Tree Wisdom*.[2]

Alternatively, you can just go for a walk and see which tree draws you. Here are a few thoughts about tree symbolism to get you started. Hazel is associated with Air. It is a good conductor of energy and is also good at detecting it – hence its use in Water divining. Holly is ruled by the element of Fire and if you think of its red berries and how its prickly leaves can hurt and sting, this makes sense. Holly is a tree of the winter season. It is associated with the energy of the old, wise, winter God. Being an evergreen it brings the energy of hope, but also the warlike energy of Mars. Holly is a tree that fights back. Another Fire tree is rowan or mountain ash with its red berries. There are many magical folk tales about how rowan can protect us against Witches, but like many folk tales, the truth is the reverse. Rowan is often used for Witches' wands.

In Britain, a tree that is associated with the element of Water is the beautiful willow with its long waving hair-like branches which trail in rivers and streams. This is a tree associated with the Goddess and the Moon. Women often like willow wands. These are all traditional European woods, but another good wood for wands is eucalyptus, which is a water-loving tree. We have a eucalyptus wand which we made for an initiation ritual in Australia.

Oak is a very 'earthy' tree. Wisdom is attributed to it because of its longevity. Oaks provide a sense of security, continuity and safety. In summer you can hide in them, as did Charles I when fleeing from the revolutionary Parliamentary forces. Oaks are amazingly prolific and represent the fecund aspect of earth. The only reason the landscape is not totally covered with oak

trees is that acorns are not very sensible about where they root themselves. Many are destroyed before they become established trees. Oak is also associated with the planet Jupiter and is thus a wood which brings good fortune. It is associated with the season of Midsummer and with kingship.

FINDING A WAND

1. To cut a wand from a tree, first find your tree. Avoid cutting wood if you can. If there is newly-fallen wood underneath the tree that has not rotted, you can take it. If you need to cut a small branch from a tree, spend some time in meditation near it. Then make sure to approach the tree with respect. Explain what you want it for and ask for the tree's permission. Then cut it calmly and as cleanly as possible. Take only what you need.

2. If on the first time you go to look for your wand, nothing strikes you as being quite right, there is plenty of time to carry on looking.

3. Once you have found your proto-wand, you must fashion and carve it to your liking. Some people carve intricate and detailed patterns, shapes and symbols on their Wands. Others prefer to adapt only slightly the natural beauty of the wood they have found. There is no right or wrong way. Do what feels most appropriate. Generally however, some working of the wood is a good idea as this starts to make it truly yours and thus, potentially, a more powerful magical tool.

CONSECRATING A WAND

1. Now you have your wand, you must devise a small ritual to consecrate it. Write some words which offer the wand to the Gods as a tool for the channelling of their energy and power. Ask them to help you use your wand wisely and well. You could say something like:

Lady of Enchantment, Lord of the Greenwood,
I offer to you this wand,
a channel of energy and power.
Grant that I may use it wisely and well,
in accordance with your will.
So mote it be!

Decide where you are going to keep your wand and find something to wrap it in – a piece of silk or woollen material would be appropriate.

2. On a day when the Moon is between New and Full, set up an altar with incense, candle, water and earth. Open your chakras and channel energy into your hands. Consecrate your wand with the elements by passing it through the incense smoke of Air, passing it swiftly through a candle flame, sprinkling it with water and then pressing it against Earth. As you pass the wand through each element, ask the element to bless your wand and the energy you will channel through it. Now say your words of dedication.

3. Hold your wand and point it above the altar. Channel energy into your hands and down the wand. Visualize the tip of the wand glowing with your energy and power. Now draw a pentagram in the air above the altar with your new wand. The invoking pentagram of Fire is best. Visualize it as a red glow emerging from the end of your wand. The pentagram looks like this:

Invoking Pentagram of Fire

Point 2 is the point of Fire. The first line of the pentagram is drawn towards the point of Fire to activate it. Then proceed through points 3–6. This first line is then sealed by going over it once more at the end. The pentagram is then completed on the point of Fire.

4. Visualize this pentagram for as long as you can and then banish it by drawing the banishing pentagram. Visualize a glowing red pentagram hanging in the air above the altar before you. Now place your wand on the Fire point and go back from point 7 to point 1 again; withdrawing the red lines of energy back into your wand.

5. Now close down your chakras and extinguish your altar lights and incense. Wrap up your wand and put it away. Make notes on this, your first simple ritual. What did you feel, see? How do you feel now the ritual is done?

Notes

1. Robert Graves, *The White Goddess*, Faber, London 1961 ed.

2. Jacqueline Memory Paterson, *Tree Wisdom: The definitive guidebook to the myth, folklore and healing power of trees*, Thorsons 1996.

8

SABBAT RITES

Witches celebrate the eight seasonal festivals of Wicca and also the thirteen Full Moons. They are a time to worship the Gods and to do magical work. A good way to start to become familiar with ritual is to create eight seasonal rites over the course of the year. In this way, you will harmonize your life with the rhythms of Nature and of the cosmos. In this harmony, you may find a source of inner peace to sustain you through life's difficulties. It may seem strange that creating your own simple ritual practices can do this. Maybe it will work for you, maybe not; but the challenge is to try it and see. A first step is to make a first seasonal altar. This is the beginning of your attunement to the cycles and rhythms of Nature. A second step is to begin to create seasonal rites.

To establish a magical routine in our lives we have to overcome that all too human failing – inertia. It can be amazingly difficult to come home from work, prepare our ritual space and perform a rite. If we force ourselves through the barrier, however tired or flat we feel beforehand, most rites will change all this. We will emerge energized and centred.

AN ORAL TRADITION

There is a lot to learn in Wicca and it could take many lifetimes. Learning is important. Wicca, like ancient Druidry, is an oral tradition that does not depend on the written word. Many people today find the idea of memorizing anything intimidating – we are a paper-bound culture. This was not the case for our magical ancestors for whom memory was more accessible than books. The Druids as the Celtic priesthood would spend 20 years committing to memory the songs, history and magic of their people. Spiritual teachings were too sacred to be written down in everyday script and had to be learned. This meant that as long as one Druid lived, then the learning of the people would be safe. Nowadays we cannot learn the sum total of all knowledge. However, in Wicca we are expected to know ritual and spells by heart. This is important. We cannot do magic while reading. The activities involve different sides of the brain. At first this seems daunting. Just learn a bit each time. After a while you will be able to learn complex rites without difficulty. There are also practical reasons why we need to know our rituals. Outdoors at night, it is impossible to read and, even indoors, it is impossible to maintain the slight trance-like state of consciousness necessary for magical ritual while engaging in a left-brain activity like reading. If you do not feel you can remember everything at once, then do some practice rituals, learning a bit at a time, until you have it all in your head.

Once we know our rituals, we can concentrate on creating the right magical energies. Repetition is therefore important. We do these simple ritual actions time and again until they become second nature. Gradually all that we have learned, visualization, meditation, ritual words and gestures, starts to come together. By building up our ritual technique bit by bit, things fall into place.

Repetition is important for other reasons. There are traditional words that are used in Wiccan ritual, but we are not bound by these. We can write our own, or we can make them up spontaneously as we go along. Different groups and individuals have different preferences. However, *morphic resonance* is an important concept for understanding how ritual works. *Morphic resonance* is the term coined by biologist Rupert Sheldrake[1] to explain the phenomenon that every species appears to have a collective or group memory which each individual of the species can access. This is true not only for biological species, but for groups of crystals, molecules and cells. Once a substance has crystallized in a certain way, or a species has made an evolutionary leap, every member of the same substance or species is likely to experience the same sort of changes. This explains a well-known scientific fact: when something has been done once in the world it can be done more easily a second time, and even more easily as time goes on. For instance, when a new drug is crystallized from a supersaturated solution, this is slow and difficult. It may take months. The next time the substance is crystallized, it happens more quickly and easily. There will be a 'past memory' to draw on. This is a more convincing explanation for this phenomenon than that put forward by some scientists: that fragments of previous crystals are transferred from laboratory to laboratory on the beards of migrating chemists.[2]

Morphic resonance is a similar idea to what psychologist Carl Jung called the *collective unconscious*, the group mind of humanity. The collective unconscious is the level at which we lose partly our individual separateness and merge our minds with those of others. Plants called rhizomes appear separate, but deep beneath the soil is a common root. At the everyday conscious level, human beings are separate, but there is a deeper

consciousness in which we are connected. It is via this deeper level of ourselves that clairvoyance, telepathy and precognition occur. In some people the door between the conscious and unconscious mind is permanently open. They are constantly aware of all sorts of unseen thoughts and energies around them. Others can open and close that door at will. In some of us, the door only opens when there is great danger or emotion. Thus people who are never normally clairvoyant may have strong premonitions if a loved one is in danger, particularly when there is a deep connection such as between parent and child.

The knowledge hidden within the collective unconscious is available to us all. What has been done once by a human being somewhere can be more easily done by others elsewhere. This means, of course, that we can communicate information between our own species in ways that are not yet understandable by science. It confirms telepathy. It also means that the sum total of human knowledge is where Witches have always said it was – within us.

Rituals themselves are fields of energy. This is why we are often attracted to ancient and archaic rituals. Rituals that have been performed repeatedly in the past have an energy and a memory of their own. For many newcomers to Wicca, its rituals are both new and yet familiar; novel but somehow not. It is as though we have been there before. While the words used by different traditions may vary, or we may create our own, the archetypal ritual pattern of the circle guarded by the four quarters, into which the powers of Goddess and God are invoked, seems ancient and deeply rooted. By the process of morphic resonance, when we perform our rites we connect ourselves with all those who have performed them before – a stream of spiritual ancestry. We in our turn are adding to the collective memory field of the rites and others in their turn will draw on our experience when they in future generations perform their rituals.

CREATING INVOCATIONS

To create a ritual, we need to call upon or invoke the Goddess and God. An invocation is an invitation for the power of the Goddess or God to make itself manifest in the circle and in our lives. These are two invocations for the Goddess and God.

Invocation to the Goddess

Dearest Goddess, in whom we live and move and have our being,
be present now within this sacred place.
Power of the Moon and of the Evening Star
descend and bless your hidden children.
Mother of Mystery who rules the seas
and the tides of emotion within women and men,
may the flow of Thy being be present within us
guiding us to truth and love and light.
Mother of the Earth, Goddess of the green and fertile land,
show to us Thy holy vision and grant us Thy wisdom.
Hail to Thee Great Goddess, whose robe is the universe
and whose mantle is the stars!

Invocation to the God

Lord of the woodlands, Lord of the breeze;
hail to Thee, Herne, Guardian of our land.
You walk the silent night beneath the stars of Thy Goddess and Lady
and the small creatures of the night are comforted by Thy presence.
At daybreak you come forth as the Power of the Sun
bringing life and warmth to sleeping soil,
awakening the energy of the Great Mother;
calling forth from her womb flowers and trees,

fruit and grain to keep us fed.
Be our shield and our protector,
lift up Thine antlered head and hear our call.

You could use these invocations for rites and you can find
many others in books. Even better, try writing your own. How
might you create an invocation for a sabbat?

Let us think about Lammas. If we go out into the countryside, what do we see? There might be fields of ripened wheat
swaying in the breeze, waiting for the harvester to come and
cut it down. Unless the wheat has been sprayed out of all existence by agri-chemicals, there will be splashes of red poppies
and blue cornflowers against the dusty gold of the wheat.
Above may be a clear blue sky and occasional cloud. The earth
will be warm to the touch after months of sun. Maybe a sudden
summer storm might appear – black clouds and hail which
threaten to flatten the wheat. And if the wheat is lost, how will
the people be fed through the long winter? Cutting time must
come quickly before it is too late.

How might we think of the God at this time? As the tall
straight stalks of wheat reaching up to the sun; proud and in
the fullness of life? How might we think of the Goddess at this
time? As the warm earth from whose womb the corn springs
forth? As the women with sickles who in ancient times would
come and reap the wheat and separate grain from chaff to make
flour and hence bread?

From these images we can create an invocation. We can call
unto our Lord the God:

Hail Lord of the Golden Wheat
tall and proud in the Summer Sun;
Hail voice of the wind, calling his destiny,
sacrifice yourself before the will of the people.

We can call upon the Goddess:

Hail unto Thee, Great Mother of All,
Thy symbol the sickle, the taker of life,
from Thy womb, Thou bringest forth life in abundance
wheat and flower, food and beauty,
from the deep rich earth that shall be the tomb of all,
we invoke Thee.

We can meditate upon these two aspects of the life force, the Divine force of all being, entering into our circle. What do these themes mean in our own lives? What is the sacrifice we must make to go forward? What is that which as the sacrificer we must demand from life? How can the polarity of these two energies – of giving and taking – be made manifest in our lives?

This is only an example of how we might take the thoughts, images, correspondences, themes, of a particular sabbat and weave them into an invocation that is also a prayer and meditation. Now try it for yourself – take the images of the next sabbat to come and play with them in your mind. Make them your own living reality and from the centre of your heart, create words which express your feelings. These do not have to be perfectly formed poems; they are only for you and the Gods to hear. Our hesitant stumblings do not offend our Gods; as long as we make them with a pure and open heart. Where all else fails, research. Look at books about Wicca and Paganism both ancient and modern and see the inspirations that others have had. Take their words if they speak to you meaningfully and adapt them if you wish, so that they speak to you still more meaningfully. All this is part of the act of worship.

SIMPLE EXERCISES TO BEGIN

CREATING A SABBAT RITUAL

1. PREPARING FOR THE RITE

First, you must think of an appropriate theme for your sabbat. In Figure 3 in Chapter 3 there are some themes and ideas for celebrating the festivals, but they may not apply to your climate. Wherever you live you must celebrate the seasonal festivals in a way that is appropriate to your own land. If you live in the Southern hemisphere, your Midsummer will be on December 21/22 and you will need to transpose all the northern hemisphere festival dates by six months. If you live in a climate that is different from temperate Europe, then you will need to see if the seasonal festivals are appropriate, or if not adapt them.

You must prepare yourself and the place in which you are to do your rite. Clean and tidy your space. Set out your altar and magical equipment. Decorate the altar and maybe your room in a way appropriate to the season. On your altar you will need representatives of the four elements – salt for Earth, a candle or lantern for Fire, a bowl of water for Water, and burning incense for Air. You will also need a wand to cast the circle and to call upon the four quarters, and a plate or basket of cakes and a chalice of wine. Try and learn as much of the rite as you can; especially the order in which things happen. You will not be able to remember all the words the first time you perform your rite. Learn a little and each time you repeat the rite, learn a little more, until it is all in your head. Write all the words out in large handwriting onto a piece of card. This will help you remember them. It also means you will not find yourself fumbling about in the semi-darkness trying to read this book!

Prepare yourself: bath or shower, put on your robe, centre yourself, meditate. Switch off the phone.

Now centre yourself to create an inner stillness – the right conditions for consciousness change. Opening the chakras is a good way of doing this; or if your ritual is outside, you can just sit quietly for a while listening to the sounds of Nature.

Now open the rite. Say something to the Gods to state your purpose. This alerts the forces of the spiritual realm that you are there and are seeking to communicate with them. It also alerts your inner self that you are now focusing on the spiritual realm. What might you say, for instance, for Spring? What is Spring about – the awakening of life in the world? What images does this bring to your mind? Take the images and create a prayer – perhaps something like this:

O Lord, O Lady, of the greenwood and fresh springtime flowers,
I have come this night to celebrate the mysteries of Spring.
Let the creative forces of Spring awaken within me
to inspire my mind and life in the coming season.
So mote it be!

3. CREATING THE CIRCLE

Now you must cast your circle. First consecrate water. Take your wand and channel power down it from your solar plexus chakra. Place the point of the wand in the water and say some words of blessing. Here are some words you can use:

I consecrate thee, O Creature of Water,
by the Might of the Moon who rules all tides and seas,
so mote it be.

Now place the point of your wand on the salt and allow more energy to flow down your wand into the salt. Now bless the salt:

I bless thee, O Creature of Salt,
by the Power of the Earth,
for the purification of all.

Now sprinkle some salt in the water:

So mote it be.

Take your water bowl around the edge of the circle, sprinkling the water on the ground to purify the ritual space. Start at the North and walk *deosil* or clockwise around the circle until you come back to the starting point. Deosil is the direction of the Sun and raises positive energy.

Next, take your censer or incense sticks and carry these around the perimeter of your sacred space; again from North and back to North again.

4. SEALING THE SACRED SPACE FROM THE OUTSIDE WORLD

Your ritual space is cleansed, purified. Now you must create a boundary between the space and the outside world. Take your wand and go to the North of your circle. Draw energy into your base of spine chakra to replenish yourself. Channel energy down your hands and along your wand to the tip. Visualize a glowing light at the tip of the wand. Hold your wand at waist height, pointing it outwards horizontally. Visualize a glowing light and energy at the end of your wand. Now walk deosil around your circle drawing a line of light and energy in the air around the edge of your ritual space. This need not be an exact circle. You can take up the whole of your room if you wish. Some words for casting the circle are:

I draw with wand the circle round,
love be raised and power be bound.
By the Might of the Moon and the Horns of Herne,
be this sacred circle formed.
So mote it be.

5. CALLING ON THE QUARTERS

Now you must call upon the elemental energies at the four quarters to guard your rite. Before calling upon the quarters, you need to visualize a scene appropriate to the element.

Air △

Go to the East of the circle. Stand facing outwards.

Visualize yourself in a high place looking into clear blue sky, the wind blowing on your face. If you wish, imagine a gust of wind lifting you up so you float on the wind.

See, feel and hear the presence of the element, and then, when you are ready, say:

Ye Mighty Ones of the East, Powers of Air
I summon, stir and call ye up,
to guard my circle and witness my rite.

Once you have felt the presence of the elemental forces, say:

Hail and Welcome!

Fire △

Now walk deosil around the circle to the South. Stand facing outwards.

Visualize a blazing Sun which grows larger and larger until it fills all your vision. You feel its heat and flames but they warm and do not burn.

See, feel and hear the presence of the element, and then, when you are ready, say:

Ye Mighty Ones of the South, Powers of Fire
I summon, stir and call ye up,
to guard my circle and witness my rite.

Once you have felt the presence of the elemental forces, say:

Hail and Welcome!

Water ▽

Now walk deosil around the circle to the West. Stand facing outwards.

Visualize a blue-green sea. The waves crash against the shore, splashing over you. Taste and smell the salt spray as it touches your lips.

Now invoke the West and welcome the Powers of Water as before.

Earth ▽

Now walk deosil around the circle to the North. Stand facing outwards.

Visualize a standing stone within a clearing in an ancient forest. Feel the rough, lichen covered stone. Smell the musty, damp, rich smell of the Earth.

Now invoke the North and the Powers of Earth.

Once you have become more familiar with the words for calling upon the quarters, you may want to draw the elemental invoking pentagrams with your wand when you invoke them. The pentagrams are like code words which over the centuries have been used to signal to the elemental worlds that we are trying to contact them.

To make invoking pentagrams, we begin at the opposite point to the element in question. For Air we start at the top right hand point of the pentagram, the point of its opposite element, Water. To draw the pentagram, follow the direction of the arrow. Start at the right hand point and trace along the horizontal line to the left hand point and then down to the bottom right hand corner. Continue until you have completed the pentagram so you are back at your starting point. Then draw the first line again to seal the pentagram by making a sixth and final stroke. This will end the pentagram at the appropriate elemental point and will make that element active. The other pentagrams are formed using the same principle.

These are the invoking pentagrams:

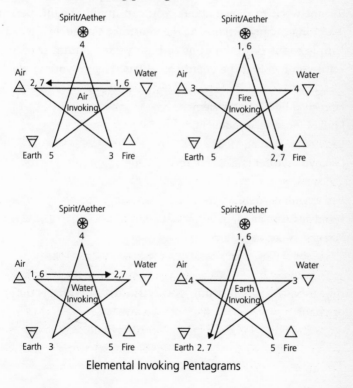

Elemental Invoking Pentagrams

The pentagrams are visualized in different colours: Air as blue; Fire as red; Water as blue-green; and Earth as brown.

6. RAISING POWER

In coven Witchcraft, the coven will frequently dance and chant at this point to raise energy for magical work. If you are working on your own, you can chant and dance in a deosil circle around your altar if it is in the centre. If your altar is in the North of the circle, try putting a small candle in the centre of your circle, perhaps within a cauldron if you have one. If you keep your eyes fixed on the flame you will find that the circling dance produces a trance effect. If you are outside and can light a fire, then this of course is the most hypnotic of all. If you do not want to dance about, you can quietly chant, perhaps watching a candle flame at the centre of the circle. Here is a simple chant. Say either one or both verses a number of times until you feel that the energy level has risen in your circle.

Hornèd Hunter, Mighty Herne,
Lord of forest, stag and night,
Lady of the shining Moon,
Lend your Power to bless my rite.

Power without and Power within,
Wand and Cup and Disc and Blade,
Fire and Water, Earth and Air,
Circle spiral, Power be raised!

If you have a small drum, you could drum while you dance or chant.

Before doing any magical work, we call upon the Divine powers of Goddess and God to bless our endeavours and to ensure that they accord with the Divine will. You can find invocations from books or write your own. The latter will helps us develop a true understanding of the nature of our Gods. Individual Witches and groups will have special God and Goddess invocations for each sabbat. As you begin to work your sabbat cycle, you can gradually build up a collection of seasonal invocations.

First, visualize an image of the Goddess you have developed from your meditations. Imagine her presence within your circle, first as a misty form and then becoming stronger and more concrete. When you can feel her energy within the circle, say your invocation. Now do the same for the God. If you have a small drum, you could drum as you invoke the God.

8. SPELLS AND MAGICAL WORK

Once we have called upon the Gods to bless our endeavours, we perform any magical work that needs to be done. Not all rituals are for magic. Especially at the sabbats, we may create a rite for worship and celebration only.

9. CELEBRATION

This is an important part of Wiccan ritual. Once we have worshipped our Gods and performed our magic, it is good to celebrate by blessing Cakes and Wine. These represent the food and sustenance that the Gods have provided for us. Offer first the cakes and then the wine to the Goddess and God, asking their blessing as you eat of their bounty.

Certain conventions apply to eating and drinking in a Wiccan circle. In a group, food is usually brought and shared. In some groups, a horn of mead is passed between the participants and

138   praises may be said to the Gods with each draft. However, a chalice of wine is more usual. As this is passed around the circle of participants, a ceremonial greeting is exchanged: 'Blessèd Be'.

The last of the cakes and wine is not consumed but is scattered and poured out on the Earth as a libation. In this way, we return of little of what we have taken. The birds usually appreciate the cake remains and an alternative is to leave them on a window sill. They will soon disappear.

10. CLOSING THE RITE

Firstly, we say a prayer of thanksgiving to the Gods for their blessing and assistance. Then we bid farewell to the quarters. We must remember that the elements are powerful forces. Whether we think of them as natural forces or as an energy within the human psyche, it is important that you do not have an excess of it wandering around in your home.

Go to each of the quarters as before, starting in the East and finishing in the North. Face outwards and address the quarters.

Ye Mighty Ones of the East (South, West, North),
Powers of Air (Fire, Water, Earth),
I thank you for attending my rite
and ere you depart to your fair and lovely realms,
I bid you: hail and farewell!

If you have used invoking pentagrams to invoke the quarters, then you should use banishing pentagrams to dismiss them. Look at the diagrams of the invoking pentagrams in Figure 18. To banish, visualize a glowing pentagram hanging in the quarter. Now place your wand on the elemental point and go back from point 7 to point 1 again; withdrawing the lines of energy back into your wand.

A final stage is to close down our energy centres, the chakras. Within the circle, we want to be as open as possible to the energies we have raised. Outside the circle we want to have control over what impinges on our psychic space.

'The rite is ended!'

Notes

1. Rupert Sheldrake, *The Rebirth of Nature: The Greening of Science and God*, Century, London 1990, page 88.
2. PV Danckwerts, (1982) Letter, *New Scientist*, *96*, pages 380–1.

GOING FURTHER

f you have got this far through this book, then take some time before going any further. Try out some of the exercises and see how well they work for you. Examine your reactions – how do they make you feel – energized, peaceful, happy, anxious, bored? If you find that these simple introductions to the world of Wicca enhance your life, then you may want to explore Witchcraft further. If so, how do you go about it?

There are many different ways, but there are four basic paths you can pursue. Two are solitary paths. One is that of the traditional Witch, otherwise known as the Wise Woman, Cunning

Man or Hedgewitch. Another solitary path is that of more modern teach-yourself Witchcraft, which you develop yourself with the aid of books and maybe attending occasional workshops or gatherings.

There are also two sorts of coven Witchcraft. One is the modern do-it-yourself variety which has flourished in the United States, often influenced by the feminist movement. Another type of coven Witchcraft is more structured and is often known today as *Traditional Initiatory Witchcraft* or sometimes *Traditional British Witchcraft*. This involves joining a coven that is part of an initiatory tradition.

Each of the four paths has a slightly different starting point. Hedgewitchery is less about ritual (though it does not abandon this completely) but is more about the Craft of the Witch. If you want to follow this path, a good starting point is Rae Beth's beautiful book *Hedgewitch*.[1] Another useful book is Marian Green's *A Witch Alone*.[2] Another skill you will need on this path is the traditional one of herbalism. There are many good books on herbalism and training is available through reputable schools of medical herbalism. You will also need to know a lot about traditional country weather lore and an enthusiasm for gardening will be a help. This path is the way of the country dweller, or those who would like to be.

The do-it-yourself method is one which has been developed in modern times. British Witch Doreen Valiente, who I hope will forgive me for describing her as one of the 'grand old ladies of the Witchcraft world', was one of the first advocates of the approach that you did not need to join a coven to be a Witch but could train yourself. She has written a whole collection of helpful books including *Witchcraft for Tomorrow*[3] which bridge the gap between traditional Craft and modern approaches. American male Witch Scott Cunningham, who died a few years ago, was a modern advocate of this approach.

His books, which include *Living Wicca: A Further Guide for the Solitary Practitioner*,[4] are widely available, particularly in the United States. He was also an expert on making incense.

Solo Witchcraft is somewhat different from the initiatory traditions and requires much less ceremonial. People on this path will often perform a ceremony of self-dedication, however, by which they offer themselves to the Gods as their vessel to do their will in the world.

If you have a group of friends who want to create a coven, but do not want to join one of the initiatory traditions, the American Witch Starhawk's famous book *The Spiral Dance*[5] describes coven practice in a modern eclectic feminist oriented coven. Starhawk's approach focuses on social, political and psychological issues. Doreen Valiente's books are also useful for those forming groups.

For those who prefer a more structured approach and want to learn from people more experienced than themselves, then initiation into one of the Witchcraft traditions is the best route. For more information about this type of Witchcraft, I suggest you read my book: *Wicca: The Old Religion in the New Millennium*.[6] This describes Wicca as an initiatory Mystery Tradition for men and women.

Some traditional initiatory groups call themselves simply 'Traditional'. Others follow traditions derived from particular covens in the UK. These include the Gardnerian tradition, named after Gerald Gardner, one of the revivers of modern Wicca, and the Alexandrian tradition named after the famous witch and magician Alex Sanders. Gardnerian and Alexandrian Witchcraft are practised throughout Europe, North America and other parts of the world. Continental Europe has some other traditions. *Greencraft* is an Alexandrian-based tradition which is more oriented towards Celtic teaching than English Alexandrian Craft. The *Celtsun* tradition is based in Germany and is a Gardnerian-derived tradition which draws on both Celtic Witchcraft and teachings from Native American spirituality and shamanism. North America has many traditional and non-traditional groups, too numerous to mention here. However a comprehensive listing of over 200 of these is available in Margot Adler's invaluable book *Drawing Down the Moon.*[7]

There are slight differences in terminology between the four different branches of Witchcraft. The word *Wicca* applied originally only to Gardnerian and Alexandrian initiatory coven Witchcraft. Today, possibly because *Wicca* is a more socially acceptable word than *Witchcraft*, in America Wicca is used to refer to all kinds of Witchcraft, much of it self-taught. This usage has now spread into Europe and elsewhere. Some British traditions think of *Wicca* as a rather New Agey and new-fangled word and prefer the good old-fashioned no-nonsense *Witchcraft* or *the Craft*.

GROUPS AND SOLO

Even if we want to join a group, it is also good to practise our ritual work alone. The feeling of being in sacred space created by ourselves is wonderful. It is also good to interact with others. There is a very special magic in working with a group of people and seeing something emerge which is much greater than the sum of the parts. The solitary path can be just that – solitary. It is helpful to be able to share our inner hopes and aspirations with others of like mind and to have friends with similar beliefs. This may not involve joining a group. In most countries where Wicca is well-developed, there are opportunities to attend the occasional gathering or workshop.

INITIATORY TRADITIONS

An important part of Wicca is that of the ancient Pagan mysteries – a way to inner transformation. There has always been exoteric religion, the religion of the state and of public temples. However, behind this were rites, ceremonies, mysteries, that were available to those who sought mystical union with the Divine and to transform their innermost being. This is the way of initiation.

There are many types of initiation. One is the initiatory process that is part of all our lives; the painful path of growth and change which life and the Divine force within us demand. This is ongoing until the day we die. There is also another form of initiation – initiation into a magical or spiritual tradition whereby we are 'grafted onto' its group mind.

We do not need to be initiated or to join a group or be trained by others to be a Witch. We can make our own spells and rituals and, if our magical ability and spiritual intent are good, they will work. However, an important principle in Witchcraft and magic is that 'old is good'. Spells that have been used time upon time and rituals which have been repeated regularly build up an energy of their own. The first few times a particular rite is performed, it is always difficult. The pattern is lacking. If a rite is repeated by different people all over the world, it becomes easier and easier. This is why all magical and spiritual traditions have their formulae – chants, spells, rites, songs – that have been repeated throughout the centuries.

This takes us back to morphic resonance. As well as each species having its own morphic field, so too do particular groups. These are called *social morphic fields*. The traditional tribe passes on its cultural patterns in this way. The living are inheritors of the memories of the dead. This is also true in other types of social organization. Members of a particular initiatory tradition are a spiritual rather than a genetic tribe who belong to the morphic field of the tradition. By being initiated into a tradition, we access its group mind and become, as it were, at one with it. We can access its inner knowledge, not only through direct teaching but unconsciously through our participation in its rites.

Many Witches believe they are reincarnated Witches of the past. Gerald Gardner believed that past Witches would be drawn back to the Craft and if we are all part of a social field then this is likely. Of course, all this is speculation not fact, but interesting speculation all the same.

Most Wiccan traditions have three levels of initiation. Before the first degree, some covens also have a neophyte initiation. This involves a period of dedication and training. The would-be witch will attend sabbats with the coven and get to know them, so that both coven and trainee can see if they are mutually suited. At the first initiation or degree, the individual is initiated as a priest or priestess and witch. After further training, there is a second initiation and the initiate becomes a High Priest or Priestess, a teacher and initiator of others. At this stage the experienced witch may start his or her own coven or training group, either independently or as an adjunct of the mother coven. At the third degree the individual has complete independence from the mother coven. Some traditions have initiations beyond the third, but these need not concern us here.

There are benefits in an initiatory tradition. We have the opportunity to be trained and advised by others, but initiation also has dangers, not least that of ego inflation. Possessing secrets or undergoing ceremonies that are the prerogative of a privileged few can be a way for us to prop up our inadequate egos. The psychologist Carl Jung wrote in his autobiography:

There is no better means of intensifying the treasured feeling of individuality than the possession of a secret which the individual is pledged to guard. The very beginning of societal structures reveal the craving for secret organizations. When no valid secrets really exist, mysteries are invented or contrived to which privileged initiates are admitted. Such was the case with the Rosicrucians and many other societies. Among these pseudo-secrets are – ironically – real secrets of which the initiates are entirely unaware – as, for example, in those societies which have borrowed their 'secret' primarily from the alchemical tradition.[8]

If you are attracted to initiatory systems because you like achieving things and collecting 'badges', then initiatory Wicca will do you more harm than good.

Secrets can have more positive effects. They can cement groups together and give them cohesion. By demonstrating that we can keep secrets, we show that we can be trusted. If we can trust each other with the secret names of our Gods, then we can trust one another with what is important to us individually, our own personal information. Loving trust builds community which can be a great source of strength to us in our spiritual quest. What is important is that initiation and secrecy do not become an excuse for self-aggrandizement and for deriving a sense of superiority over others. Collective identities can become personas which inhibit our spiritual and magical progress rather than help them. Titles such as priest and priestess are heady enough; how much more so those of High Priest or Witch Queen. These titles are even more dangerous when they are self-conferred as has been recommended by some Wiccan books. At least if the title is conferred by a community, hopefully they have a standard by which to measure whether we are worthy of it. Otherwise it is a bit like founding one's own university and awarding oneself a doctorate. It may sound great, but what is it worth?

POWERS

If you want to develop your Wicca, then some of the skills and techniques in this book will help you. The aim of the exercises is to build up your powers of magic and clairvoyance, but also to encourage your spiritual development. As I have said before, magic in the service of the ego is a recipe for disaster. As with initiation, the powers are not ends in themselves. They are means by which we aspire to become better integrated people who can contribute to society and to the world.

Many of the systems which today we think of as mystical, such as Yoga and the Qabalah, were also systems that developed magical powers. In Yoga, these powers are called *Siddhis*. Interestingly, attractive though the idea of being able to do magic may be, the *Siddhis* were considered side effects – not ends in themselves. The aim of mysticism is union with the Divine. In systems such as Christianity that personify their Gods, the ultimate goal was to dwell in the presence of God. In most branches of Hinduism, it was to become at one with the Divine. Here the Divine is a state of inner being – a state of consciousness, awareness or bliss. In Wicca, the Goddess promises that at the end of our spiritual journey:

Before my face belovèd of Gods and men
thine inmost Divine self
shall be enfolded in the rapture of the infinite.

This tells us many things – that behind the forms of the Gods there is a greater existence. Here it is called Goddess but at this level we are beyond the distinctions of male and female, beyond polarity and personification. We enter the realms of the One, the Life Force, the Source of all being. Paradoxically, this One is also All. All life springs from it and as the Goddess says:

From me all things proceed
and unto me all things must return...

In mysticism, then, we return to our source.

Enraptured and enfolded in the arms of the belovèd,
Sister and bridegroom of my soul,
father and mother of my flesh,
twin being of my spirit,
I enter Thy embrace.

Deity is immanent and transcendent. We can see material creation as a mountain of which the Divine is the peak – or as a journey to the Centre of the Earth with the Divine at the core and centre.

Entering matter we journey
and experience all creation,
interconnected, One.

As the famous Greek philosopher Heraclitus, who originated in the Goddess' sacred city of Ephesus, said in about 500 BCE:

The way up and the way down –
is one and the same.

A NEW AND OLD RELIGION

Magic and Paganism survived in two levels of society: amongst the educated classes and amongst country people who tilled the land. The former was a Paganism mingled with ritual magic. The latter was the folk magic, Witchcraft and Pagan traditions that were part of agricultural life. It was when these two strands reunited that Wicca revived. High magic that is intellectual and disconnected from Nature can be joyless and sterile. Traditional Witchcraft unenlightened by a sound ethical base and spiritual development can degenerate into a series of self-serving magical technologies. United they can form a coherent spiritual philosophy ideally suited to our postmodernist society.

Wicca is often called the *Old Religion* but while it emphasizes its continuity with ancient Pagan traditions, Wicca is a path for people living in today's world. Many people are looking for a new spiritual vision that can take them forward into the twenty-first century. Religious traditions based on racist, sexist and speciesist assumptions are spiritually bankrupt and of as much use as a 286 computer. This does not mean that we must discard all that we have learned and evolved over the past millennia. Today we are fortunate heirs of many thousands of years of human culture and thought. The power of mass communications and the migration of peoples around the globe, sometimes voluntary and sometimes forced, means we are in the fortunate position of being able to access not only our own cultures, but many others. Human reason has given us the power to discriminate. We do have some control over our destinies and some freedom to choose the belief systems and philosophies that govern our lives. And, if many people now make right choices, if they choose paths which emphasize love of one another and of the whole of creation, then a sufficient mass weight of opinion will build up to change for the better the societies in which we live.

The Witch does not separate him- or herself from politics or from the existing order. Instead, we seek to change it. We take social action; we perform eco-magic; we petition our Gods; and we try and transform ourselves so that we drop ideas like pearls into the sea of the collective human psyche. In Wicca the

Divine is immanent or indwelling in this world. We seek to
know the Divine, not by withdrawing from the world, but by
engaging with it. Enlightenment and union with the Divine can
be found in everyday life and in the world around us. It is not
reserved for some non-material and transcendent realm.

Not only Witches but many others have looked at our modern
world and realized that new forms of spirituality would be necessary in the coming millennium. The psychologist Carl Jung
foresaw many of the religious developments that have occurred
in Wicca and Paganism today. No longer would we worship a
male trinity, instead the feminine and the Goddess would be
incorporated into our ideas of the Divine. The balance of fourness
– the opposites held in tension would be important; as in the four
elements of Wicca and other Pagan traditions. The Divine would
be both 'Father' and 'Mother', or 'Son' and 'Daughter'. The
Divine would be not only in 'heaven' but on 'Earth', immanent or
in-dwelling in matter. We would honour the Divine in Nature
and in the human body as well as in the realms beyond.

Carl Jung believed that with the coming of the Age of
Aquarius an upheaval would occur in the human psyche. The
archetypes which governed the Piscean era would be over-
thrown. All over the world people would be gripped by inner
visions that would result in new religious images for the
human community. The Jungian analyst Dr Max Zeller once
related a dream of his to Carl Jung:[9]

A temple of vast dimensions was in the process of being built.
As far as I could see – ahead, behind, right and left – there were
incredible numbers of people building on gigantic pillars. I, too,
was building on a pillar. The whole building process was in its
very beginnings, but the foundation was already there, the rest of
the building was starting to go up, and I and many others were
working on it.[10]

This is how Jung interpreted the dream.

> ...that is the temple we all build on. We don't know the people because, believe me, they build in India and China and in Russia and all over the world. That is the new religion.
>
> 'You know how long it will take until it is built?'
>
> I said, 'How should I know? Do you know?'
>
> He said, 'I know.'
>
> I asked how long it would take.
>
> He said, 'About six hundred years.'
>
> 'Where do you know this from?' I asked.
>
> He said, 'From dreams. From other people's dreams and from my own. This new religion will come together as far as we can see.'[11]

This would take us forward to about 2,550 CE.

In this vision, spiritual renewal would come not from orthodox structures and religious hierarchies. It would come from where it has always originated – from those with no vested interest in the power structures of the time. Each new tradition has given way when it has been outgrown, but never without a fight. Each spiritual visionary has been a heretic amongst his or her own people; just as those today who question the past and are trying to create a spiritual vision for the future are outside the existing orthodoxies.

The source of spiritual vision is deep within us; within the heart, mind, soul and spirit. In our era we are seeing a shift of

152 authority away from outside authorities to within the individual. There is no centralized and orthodox version of deity to which all must subscribe; instead we have the spiritual reality of today, which is *pluralism*: there are many paths, many ways, many visions of the Divine. What members of this new spiritual community share is a common commitment to the Sacred Quest – for wholeness within and for social, community and planetary responsibility. However, each one of us is free to experience our own religious symbols and to create a personal spirituality based on understanding the true nature of the holistic universe. For some, this will be the path of Wicca.

THE END

Today, many have answered the call of the Goddess and of the Lord of the Woods to build a new spiritual vision for the Age to come. So this book is theirs, although I cannot hope to fully tell their story; but we who share it will in the coming years dance it, sing it and little by little, word by word, come nearer to the truth.

Remember: Wicca is a way of being, of life, of love, of joy, of laughter, of accepting that life can be painful and tough, while doing what we can to make it a better place for others and for ourselves.

Be blessed, be happy, be wise,
laugh and love!
This is the way of Goddess and God.
Blessèd Be!

1. Rae Beth, *A Guide to the Solitary Practitioner*, Hale 1990.

2. Marian Green, *A Witch Alone*, Aquarian, London 1991.

3. Doreen Valiente, *Witchcraft for Tomorrow*, Hale, London 1978.

4. Scott Cunningham, *Living Wicca: A Further Guide for the Solitary Practitioner*, Llewellyn 1996.

5. Starhawk, *The Spiral Dance: A Rebirth of the Ancient Religion of the Great Goddess*, 2nd ed, Harper and Row, San Francisco 1989.

6. Vivianne Crowley, *Wicca: The Old Religion in the New Millennium*, 2nd ed, Thorsons 1996.

7. Margot Adler, *Drawing Down the Moon: Witches, Druids, Goddess-Worshippers and other Pagans in America Today*, Arkana/Penguin, 1997 ed. This is an excellent survey of North American Paganism with extensive lists of organizations and magazines.

8. CG Jung, *Memories, Dreams and Reflections*, recorded and edited by Aniela Jaffé and trans by R and C Winston, Fontana Paperback, 1995 ed, first English language edition 1961, pages 375–6.

9. Max Zeller, (1975) The task of the analyst, *Psychological Perspectives*, 6, 1, pages 74–8.

10. Zeller (1975), page 75.

11. Zeller (1975), page 75.

GROUPS AND CONTACTS

I t is important to remember that you do not have to become a Witch! This is not a path suitable for everybody. Wicca is a *vocation*, a calling. It is right for some and not for others. You do not have to be psychic or have great magical powers. You do need a love of the Gods, a desire to serve them and a feeling that you have been called by them.

Anyone considering Wicca should also look at what other Pagan groups and other traditions such as Druidry have to offer. A Druid contact address is given below. There are many Pagan groups which share the same festival cycle as Wicca, but are less intense and may have slightly different emphases – e.g. Goddess rather than Goddess and God, meditative practice rather than ritual. If you want to find out something about other Pagan paths, you can read my book *Principles of Paganism*.[1] There are also ritual magic groups which are dedicated to spiritual progression. Some of these, particularly those deriving from the nineteenth-century magical group *The Golden Dawn*, may be fairly Pagan. Others are based on the Judaic mysticism of the Qabalah. However, in recent years, some qabalistic groups have become Pagan-oriented.

COVENS AND GROUPS

Wiccan covens vary in their emphasis according to the interests of their members. These could range from worship, magic, revival of folk medicine, Celtic tradition, spiritual development, ritual magic and healing to environmental action. If you are a dedicated environmentalist you may feel frustrated with a group which is focused on healing or personal transformation and vice versa.

If you decide that you want to join a group, it is important to remember that Wicca requires a high level of dedication. Most groups are small and depend on most of their members being there most of the time. You will feel guilty and may be disruptive if you cannot match their commitment. Do not be afraid to ask how often a group meets – monthly, fortnightly, weekly – and if you are expected to study in between.

Be realistic about what you can do. Do you have transport (I do not mean a broomstick)? If not, will you really want to travel 50 miles with three changes of train on a Wednesday night in the middle of January? Can you really cope with the coven's study programme and your university degree? If the answer is no, then it is better to join something less demanding or to practise solo until time and circumstances are right. You do not want to decide that you were being unrealistic after you have been initiated. This is unfair both to the group and to you.

Do you have a non-Wiccan partner? How will he or she regard your new-found path? How will your partner feel about you going off to your new friends and leaving him or her alone? Will your relationship stand the strain? What does the group consider secret and how much can you tell your partner? Does the group work skyclad and what will your partner think about this? If these issues are not resolved, much heartache can result afterwards.

In all spiritual paths, there are groups and individuals who exploit others for their own ends. There are surprisingly few of these in Wicca compared with other spiritual traditions; but this does not mean that abuses could never occur. Use your intuition. If you have doubts about anyone who describes themselves as Wiccan or a Witch, do not become involved with them. Beware of those who claim great powers, or to be inheritors of secret traditions, but whose everyday lives are a mess. If they cannot organize their own lives, then they are not the ideal people to be guiding your spiritual and magical progress.

Beware also of those who suggest that sex might form part of your initiation ceremony. It might be a traditional part of their ancient induction ceremony and it may seem a romantic idea at the time, but will you still think so in a year or two? Use your common sense. If on initial acquaintance people seem to be on an ego trip, they probably are, and any group they run will be dysfunctional. Ask what happens if you want to leave the group. Ask who has left in the past and why? In other words, if you are an enthusiastic seeker, do not let your enthusiasm make you naive!

CONTACTING GROUPS

If you are seeking a group, these are some addresses you can write to which may help you. These groups are all run by contributions from volunteers. This means that you must send postage if you want a reply. When writing to organizations in your own country, unless the individual listings give contrary information, please send an SAE. If you are writing to organizations in other countries, do not send stamps because they cannot use them. Instead send International Reply Coupons (IRCs) which you can buy from large post offices. These can be exchanged for stamps anywhere in the world. Alternatively, if you cannot obtain IRCs, send a donation in your own currency.

If no organization is listed for your own country, contact one of the larger organizations in Britain and Ireland or the USA. They may be able to help you.

EUROPE

Aradia Trust, BM Deosil, London WC1N 3XX provides information on Wicca in the UK. For its booklet *Wicca in Britain*, please send cheque or postal order for £2 made payable to *The Aradia Trust*.

Cauldron available from Mike Howard, Caemorgan Cottage, Caemorgan Road, Cardigan, Dyfed, SA43 1QU, Wales, UK, is an informative journal of the Old Religion and one of the oldest Craft magazines. *Cauldron* is especially useful for those interested in solo or coven Traditional Witchcraft.

Circe, Postbus 2191, 3500 GD Utrecht, The Netherlands, provides contacts in the Netherlands and Craft supplies.

Circle du Dragon, BP 68, 33034 Bordeaux Cédex, France – EMail: troisp@hol.fr – has a magazine and can assist with training.

Marian Green, BCM-SCL QUEST, London WC1N 3XX, is a magician in the Western Ways who runs courses in Natural Magic and produces *Quest* magazine. *Quest* has an annual conference.

Greencraft België vzw, p/a Lange Lozannastraat 43, 2018 Antwerpen, Belgium – EMail: JanDZ@mail.dma.be – is a foundation representing a number of Alexandrian covens in Belgium, The Netherlands and the state of Texas, most of which provide training. Greencraft also publishes a quarterly magazine.

Nordic Pagan Federation, (Nordisk Paganist Forbund) PO Box 1814, Nordnes, 5024 Bergen, Norway – EMail: pagan@bgnett.no – Web site: http://www.bgnett.no/pagan/ – can provide information on Wicca in Scandinavian countries.

Pagan Federation, BM Box 7097, London WC1N 3XX, England, is the main Pagan body in Europe. There is a magazine *Pagan*

Dawn which lists groups, courses, conferences, contact networks, social meetings, etc, in Britain and other parts of Europe, covering all Pagan paths including Wicca. The magazine is £8 pa. Also PF Scotland, PO Box 932, Edinburgh, EH17 7PW, Scotland. The PF's web site – http://www.paganfed.demon.co.uk – gives information and lists events.

School of Living Arts e.v., Zornstrasse 11a, 67549 Worms, Germany, can provide information on German Wicca networks and workshops.

Wiccan Rede, PO Box 473, Zeist, NL 3700 AL, The Netherlands; EMail: silver.circle@tip.nl – is an English/Dutch Wiccan magazine which can assist with contacts in the Netherlands.

Wicca Study Group, BM Deosil, London WC1N 3XX; EMail: BMDEOSIL@aol.com; website: http://home.aol.com/BMDEOSIL is run by Vivianne and Chris Crowley. The WSG runs courses, retreats and workshops in the UK, Germany and France. A home study course which develops the ideas outlined in this book is available in English, French or German.

NORTH AMERICA

Adair BranDubh and Eland, PO Box 876, Station B, Ottawa, Ontario, K1P 5P9, Canada; EMail – imawitch@cyberus.ca – can offer advice on contacting initiatory Wicca in Canada.

Aquarian Tabernacle Church, PO Box 73, Index, Washington 98256, USA, is a Wiccan church which provides teaching in Paganism and is active in Interfaith work. There are ATC affiliated organizations in Australia.

Church of All Worlds, PO Box 488, Laytonville, CA 95454, USA – EMail: cawnemeton@aol.com – is a Pagan organization which raises ecological awareness through its subsidiary, *Forever Forests*, and publishes the magazine *Green Egg*.

Circle, PO Box 219, Mount Horeb, WI 53572, USA, organ-izes Pagan events, fosters contacts and networking, and publishes the quarterly journal *Circle Network News*. Circle publishes the *Circle Guide to Pagan Groups* which lists groups in North America and can supply books by mail order. There are gatherings, a land sanctuary, counselling service and many other activities.

Covenant of the Goddess, PO Box 1226, Berkeley, CA 94704, USA – Web site: http://www.cog.org – is a cross-traditional federation of more than 100 covens, plus solitary elders and associates who have joined together to win recognition for the Craft as a legitimate religion.

EarthSpirit, PO Box 365-N, Medford, MA 02155, USA – EMail: earthspirit@earthspirit.com – web site: http://www.earthspirit. com – is a non-profit organization providing services to a nationwide network of Pagans and other followers of earth-centred religions.

Gaia Group, Inc, PO Box 50092, Staten Island, NY 10303, USA, is an initiatory Earth Religion with Wiccan roots dedicated to the care and protection of Mother Earth through both magickal and practical means.

Hecate's Loom, Box 5206, Station B, Victoria, BC, V8R 6N4, Canada; web site: http://www.hecate.com – EMail: loom@island-net.com – is one of the largest and oldest Pagan publications in Canada. It focuses on west coast Wiccan activities.

Reclaiming, PO Box 14404, San Francisco, CA 94114, USA – EMail: reclaiming@reclaiming.org – Web site: http://www.web-com.com/cauldron/ – is a Center for Feminist Spirituality – a collective of women and men working to unify spirituality and politics. It offers workshops, summer programs, public rituals, newsletter, and is inspired by the work of Starhawk.

Wiccan Church of Canada, 109 Vaughan Road, Toronto, M6C 2L9, Canada – EMail: info@wcc.on.ca – web site: http://www. wcc.on.ca – is a network of Wiccan groups in the Odyssian tradition. It offers training, information and ritual celebrations and publishes a magazine.

AUSTRALIA AND NEW ZEALAND

Pan-Pacific Pagan Alliance, PO Box 1, Perthville, NSW 2795, Australia; and *Pan-Pacific Pagan Alliance*, PO Box 1459, Waikato Mail Centre, Hamilton, New Zealand; has a members' magazine *Pagan Times* which lists groups, contacts and events. The magazine is available from The Editor, PO Box 1800, Tuggeranong, ACT 2601, Australia. The PPPA's website is – http://www.summit.fl.net.au/pppa/ – and has lots of useful information including current magazine prices.

OTHER ORGANIZATIONS WHICH MAY BE OF INTEREST

Dragon, 39 Amersham Road, London SE14 6QQ, England; EMail: Adrian@gn.apc.org; website: http://www.coventry. demon.co.uk/esprit/drag1.html, is a network combining eco-magic with practical conservation and campaigning. Events are organized across Britain. Dragon produces *Dragon Diary* eight times a year and a twice-yearly magazine.

Fellowship of Isis, Clonegal Castle, Clonegal, Enniscorthy, Ireland or EMail: isis@cerbernet.co.uk – is a world-wide Goddess organization, many of whose members belong to other Pagan or Wiccan groups and organizations. Some of its members run *Iseums*, Goddess groups, which meet regularly. There is provision for training in the Goddess priesthood. The FOI has a magazine, *Isian News*. The FOI also runs the *Druid Clan of Dana* which has a magazine *Aisling* available from PO Box 196, London WC1N 3XX, England. The *Fellowship of Isis* itself is run from the home of the Hon. Olivia Durdin-Robertson.

Invisible College, PO Box 42, Bath, BA1 1ZN, England, teaches all aspects of the Western Mystery Tradition (of which the Craft is a part) including ritual arts, the Grail Mysteries, folk healing and much more. Teaching is provided through short courses and by post.

Order of Bards, Ovates and Druids, PO Box 1333, Lewes, BN7 3ZG, England; website – http://www.obod.co.uk – is the largest Druid order in Europe. It also has groups in North America. OBOD offers training in Druidry covering healing, divination, mythology, history and folklore through correspondence course, workshops and retreats in Europe and the United States. There is a members' magazine and regular events. Many of its members also belong to other Pagan or Wiccan groups.

Scientific and Medical Network, Gibliston Mill, Colinsburgh, Leven, Fife, Scotland, KY9 1JS, UK – EMail: SciMedNetwork@ compuserve.com – is not a Pagan organization but may be of interest to scientists with Wiccan interests. It is an international grouping of scientists, academics, engineers, therapists and medical practitioners who are working to bridge the gap between science and mysticism. It runs interesting conferences and events.

Talking Stick, PO Box 3719, London SW17 8XT, England, is the high quality quarterly magazine of the *Talking Stick* esoteric discussion forum which meets fortnightly in a Central London pub. This is well worth a visit for visitors to London.